NEW EDITION

BUSINESS OBJECTIVES

Vicki Hollett

Oxford University Press

Contents

1 MEETING PEOPLE PAGE 6

TOPICS	LANGUAGE	VOCABULARY/PRONUNCIATION	SKILLS WORK
Getting information Describing jobs Commuters Personality profile	Introductions Prepositions – jobs *Wh-* question forms Present Simple tense *How long does it take?*	Countries and nationalities Word stress	SPEAKING 1: The Conference Game WRITING: A personal profile SPEAKING 2: Organizing your studies

2 TELEPHONING PAGE 16

TOPICS	LANGUAGE	VOCABULARY/PRONUNCIATION	SKILLS WORK
Starting calls Transferring information Deciding what to do Requests	*Can /could /may I... ?* *Can / could / would you... ?* Instant decisions: *I'll...*	Telephone language *lend* and *borrow* Spelling the alphabet Telephone numbers	LISTENING: Messages SPEAKING: Two telephone role-plays WRITING: Business letters

3 COMPANIES PAGE 28

TOPICS	LANGUAGE	VOCABULARY/PRONUNCIATION	SKILLS WORK

Company profiles
Facilities
Organizations
Current activities
Company strengths
	Present Continuous
	   and Present Simple tenses
	Has got
	It is / There is / There are
		Company departments
		
		-s endings: /s/, /z/, /ɪz/
		Numbers
			LISTENING: A presentation of BICC
			SPEAKING: Presenting your
			   company

4 EXCHANGING INFORMATION PAGE 38

TOPICS	LANGUAGE	VOCABULARY/PRONUNCIATION	SKILLS WORK

Description
Explaining what you need
Size and dimension
Sorting words
	Adjectives
	was and *were*
	What was it like?
	Dimensions
	It weighs / costs...
		Sorting and recording new
		   vocabulary
		
		Words with different spellings
		   that sound the same
			SPEAKING 1: A crossword
			LISTENING: A sales team briefing
			SPEAKING 2: Executive toys

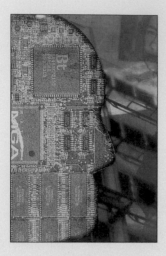

OBJECTIVE

to meet foreign
contacts and get to
know them

TASKS

to introduce yourself
to other people

•

to describe jobs and
responsibilities

•

to find out about other
people's jobs

•

to ask questions about
foreign companies

•

to read and write a
personal profile

PRESENTATION

1 Do you know the other people in the class? Introduce yourself to
everyone.

Good morning. My name is ... and I work for / in ... .

2 Look at the people in the photographs.

1 Is it a formal or informal situation?
2 What are they saying?

a

b

c

3 ▭ Listen to three conversations and match each one to the correct
picture.

4 [1a] Listen to the first conversation again and complete this conversation.

Louise   Mr Velázquez, _____ ____ _____ you to Peter Brien. Peter, _____ _____ Mr Velázquez of Telefónica de España.

Mr Velázquez _____ ____ _____ _____?

Peter   _____ ____ _____ _____?

Louise   Peter works for our New York branch. He's _____ _____ international accounts.

5 [1b] Put this conversation in the right order. Write numbers in the boxes. Then listen to the second conversation again and check your answers.

☐ **Thomas**   Yes, I do. How are you, Sven?
☐ **Sven**   Not bad, thanks.
☐ **Thomas**   Welcome to Oxford. It's nice to see you again.
☐ **Thomas**   Good. Let's go upstairs and have some coffee.
☐ **Sven**   Fine thanks, Thomas. And you?
☐ **Ulla**   And you. Do you know my colleague, Sven Olsen?
☐ **Thomas**   Fine. How was your trip?

6 [1c] Listen to the third conversation again and correct the mistakes in these sentences.

> Bob, Liz and Luigi are in ~~an office.~~ a pub

1 It's the afternoon.
2 Liz and Luigi work together.
3 Luigi is in the construction business.

7 Work in groups. Practise making introductions. Introduce:

1 two people in a formal situation.
2 two people in an informal situation.
3 yourself at a company reception desk.
4 yourself to a new colleague.
5 yourself to a foreign visitor you are meeting at an airport.

May I introduce you to ... ?	... this is ...
How do you do?	How do you do?
Do you know ... ?	... this is ...
Hello. / Hi.	Nice to meet you.
Good morning. My name is ...	I have an appointment to see ...
I don't think we've met. I'm ...	
Excuse me. Are you Mrs Eustace? I'm ...	

8 When do we say *good morning*, *good afternoon*, *good evening*, and *good night*?

LANGUAGE WORK

Getting information

I Five people are visiting your company today. Look at their business cards and ask and answer questions about them.

What's his/her name?
(What is)

What nationality is he/she?

Who does he/she work for?

Where does he/she work?

What's his/her position in the company?

SKANESBANKEN

BIRGITTE SVENSSON
DEPUTY MANAGING DIRECTOR

NYBROKAJEN 7
S - 15146 STOCKHOLM
TEL: 08 663 50 40
FAX: 08 665 40 55

CHEMA Y PUNTO SA

MARGARITA VIDAL ROMERO
Public Relations Officer

PASEO DE LA CASTELLANA 201
MADRID

Tel: 1 431 2687   Fax: 1 435 1314   Telex: 45951

B S C S
BUSINESS SYSTEMS CONSULTANCY SERVICES

DALE CROSBY
VICE PRESIDENT

1049 DERWENT DRIVE SANTA BARBARA CALIFORNIA
Tel: 805 963 9171   Fax: 805 962 8593

NIHON INFORMALINK KK

Ni

Headquarters
Informalink BLDG
2-4-8 Kanamecho
Toshima-ku
Tokyo 171

Telephone: (6) 5995 3801/4
Telefax: (6) 5995 3919

NOBURO YAEGASHI
SALES REPRESENTATIVE

DEUXMONT FRANCE

JEAN-CLAUDE AURELLE
Technical Director

132 rue Véron, 94140 Alfortville, France
Telephone: (33) 1 43 76 62 81
Telefax: (33) 1 43 7629 24

2 Now find out about the people sitting next to you.

What's your name?
What nationality … ? etc.

3 Put the right question word in the spaces.

When	Where	Why	What	How	Who	Which

WELCOME TO THE CONFERENCE

…… are you here? — To find out about IPQ's newest product.

…… is it? — The RM110 data communication system.

…… many people are attending? — 76

…… are they? — European members of the IPQ team.

…… divisions do they work in? — Marketing and Sales

…… do we meet? — At 6 o'clock this evening.

…… do we meet? — In the Regency Lounge (1st floor).

IPQ

4 Here are some answers, but what are the questions?

1 How do you do?
2 José Pérez.
3 J-O-S-E.
4 I'm Spanish.
5 No, I'm single.
6 IBM.
7 They produce and sell computers.
8 The financial department.
9 I'm an auditor.
10 English, Spanish, and Italian.

All these questions are in the Present tense. For more information on the Present Simple, see page 166 in the Grammar and Usage Notes.

5 Write some questions to ask a colleague. Ask about

• their company
• their job
• their responsibilities
• their hobbies and interests.

Find someone you don't know very well and ask your questions.

Describing jobs

1 Study the words in **bold type** in these sentences.

I'm	**a** financial controller.	(**a/an** + job)
	an engineer.	
I work **for** ATT.		(**for** + employer)
I'm **in**	marketing.	(**in** + type of work)
	the chemicals business.	
	chemicals.	

Complete this conversation. Use *a*, *an*, *for*, and *in*.
A What do you do for a living?
B I'm _____ computers.
A Really? Who do you work _____?
B Olivetti. I'm _____ product manager. What about you?
A I work _____ Balfour Beatty.
B So you're _____ the construction business?
A Yes. I'm _____ engineer.

2 Complete these sentences about yourself.
1 I'm a/an _____ .
2 I work for _____ .
3 I'm in _____ .

3 How many executive managers and divisions does this organization have?

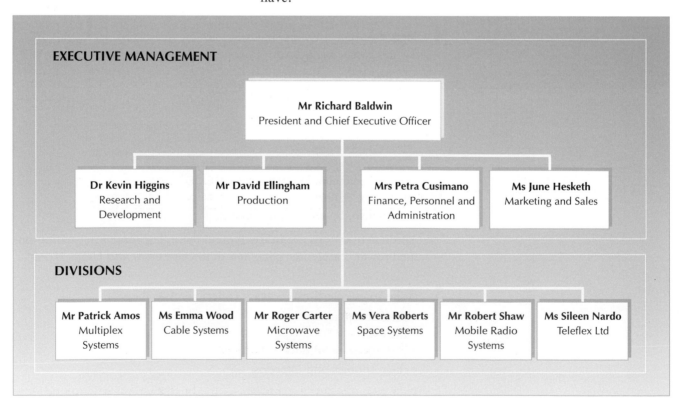

EXECUTIVE MANAGEMENT

Mr Richard Baldwin
President and Chief Executive Officer

Dr Kevin Higgins
Research and Development

Mr David Ellingham
Production

Mrs Petra Cusimano
Finance, Personnel and Administration

Ms June Hesketh
Marketing and Sales

DIVISIONS

Mr Patrick Amos
Multiplex Systems

Ms Emma Wood
Cable Systems

Mr Roger Carter
Microwave Systems

Ms Vera Roberts
Space Systems

Mr Robert Shaw
Mobile Radio Systems

Ms Sileen Nardo
Teleflex Ltd

Ask and answer questions about it.

Who is	responsible for in charge of	production?	Mr Ellingham.
Who is he responsible to? Who does he report to?		The Chief Executive Officer.	

4 Find out about your partner.
- Which division do they work in?
- What are they responsible for?
- Who are they responsible to?

Commuters

1 Ask and answer questions about these commuters.

Rosa Gonzalez, architect. Works in 42nd Street, New York. Lives 2 miles away at Central Park West and 86th Street. 15-minute journey on rollerblades. Thinks about the day ahead or listens to her personal stereo.

Matthew Long, jeweller. Works in Hatton Garden, London. Lives 4 miles away in Hornsey. 25-minute journey on bike. Has to concentrate on the traffic.

Daisuke Tanaka and Hideo Nakajima. Work for banks in Otemachi, Tokyo. Live 20 miles away in Chiba. 50-minute journey by train. Read comic books or sleep.

What does Rosa do for a living?
Where does she live?
Where does she work?
How long does it take to get there?
How far is it?
How does she get there?
What does she do on the journey?

2 Now ask a partner similar questions about their journey to work.

Countries and nationalities

1 *Toshiba is a* **Japanese** *company.   The headquarters are in* **Japan.**

               | |

        nationality   country

What about these companies?

1	Honda	6	L'Oréal
2	IBM	7	Rolls-Royce
3	Olivetti	8	Nestlé
4	Ericsson	9	Siemens
5	Norsk Hydro	10	Philips

2 Complete the chart.

Country	Nationality
Japan	Japanese
The USA	
	Italian
Sweden	
	Norwegian
France	
	British
Switzerland	
Germany	
The Netherlands	

3 Work with a partner. Say where these letters and stamps are from.
This one's from Brazil. It's Brazilian.

What other countries and organizations does your company have contact with?

Personality profile

I Read this article about a businessman called George Wong. What information is missing? Suggest possible words to fill the spaces.

PEOPLE IN FOCUS: *George Wong*

In his free time George listens to _____ [5]. He likes bands like Led Zeppelin and T Rex. He has _____ [6] cars, including a Ferrari 512TR, an Aston Martin Lagonda, a Lamborghini Diablo, three Mercedes, and a Mini. It's an unusual Mini because it has a television, fridge and _____ [7] machine inside.

George hates _____ [8]. He says he's bad at things like balance sheets and profit and loss accounts, and he also hates _____ [9]. He never wears one.

George Wong comes from _____ [1] but he lives in _____ [2]. He's _____ [3] years of age, very successful, and he loves his job. He is Chairman of Parkview, a property development, ship building, and _____ [4] business.

2 Work with a partner. One person uses the information below and the other uses the information in File 1 on page 158.

Ask your partner questions to get the information missing from the article. Complete the article.

Where does George Wong come from?
Where does he live?

Pronunciation

I 🔲 Listen to these words from Unit 1. Mark the syllable where the main stress falls.

Example   inter<u>na</u>tional

a construction
b engineer
c headquarters
d financial

e European
f responsible
g responsibilities
h nationality

2 Now practise saying the words. Make sure you stress the right syllable.

SKILLS WORK

Speaking 1

Work in twos or threes. You are participants at an international conference. Toss a coin to move.

- Heads: move one square.
- Tails: move two squares.

Follow the instructions on each square and start a conversation. The first person to finish is the winner.

You see an old friend. Greet him/her.	Name three countries which begin with the letter 'B'.	Ask another person where they come from.	Introduce two people to one another.	Ask another person about their family.
Ask another person about their company.				Name two countries where you bow when you meet someone.
Name four countries you want to visit on holiday.		THE CONFERENCE GAME		Ask another person about their hobbies and interests.
Ask another person at the conference what their job is.				Exchange business cards with another participant.
Introduce yourself to another person at the conference.				Say 'thank you' in three different languages.
You arrive at the conference hotel. Go to the reception desk and register.	← START	FINISH	It's time to go home. Say goodbye to your new friends.	Ask another person about the department or division they work in.

Writing   Read the profile of Derek Stirling and then write another profile about yourself. Use the topics below to help you.

name   company   responsibilities
nationality   position in the company hobbies
home town

PROFILE

My name is Derek Stirling and I'm Scottish. I live in Hadlow, a lovely English village near London, and I work for The Swire Group, Britain's largest private company. The Group's activities are divided into five business areas: shipping, aviation, property, industries, and trading. Our best-known company is Cathay Pacific Airways.

I work at our London head office; I'm head of Corporate Finance, and I'm responsible for developing the business of the Group.

I'm always very busy and I don't have much free time, but when I do, I like fishing and I grow my own vegetables, just for fun.

Speaking 2   Interview a partner about their learning objectives.

1 Why do they want to learn English?
2 Who do they want to communicate with in English?
3 What do they want to practise most: reading, writing, listening, or speaking?
4 How many hours a week can they spend studying English?
5 What equipment and materials do they have to help them learn?
6 What equipment and materials do they want to buy?

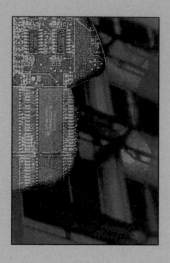

OBJECTIVE

to make contact and exchange information over the phone

TASKS

to spell and note down key words and numbers in a telephone message
•
to make, agree to, and refuse requests
•
to respond to new situations and say what action you will take
•
to write business letters confirming telephone calls

PRESENTATION

1   Study these forms. What are they for?

🖥️ Listen to the two telephone conversations and complete the forms.

Conversation 1

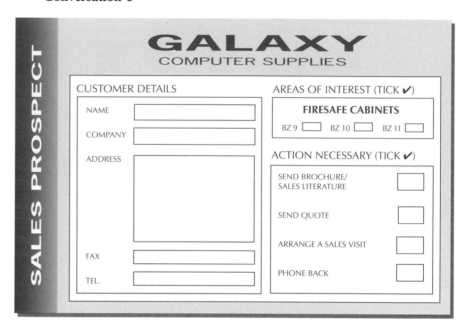

Conversation 2

2 Listen to the conversations again and answer these questions.

3a a Why doesn't the switchboard operator connect the caller immediately?

b What does the woman say she'll do?

3b c What question does Christophe Terrien ask about the photoconductor units?

d What does Mary Thatcher ask Christophe Terrien to do?

3 Match the words and phrases (1-10) with similar meanings (a-j).

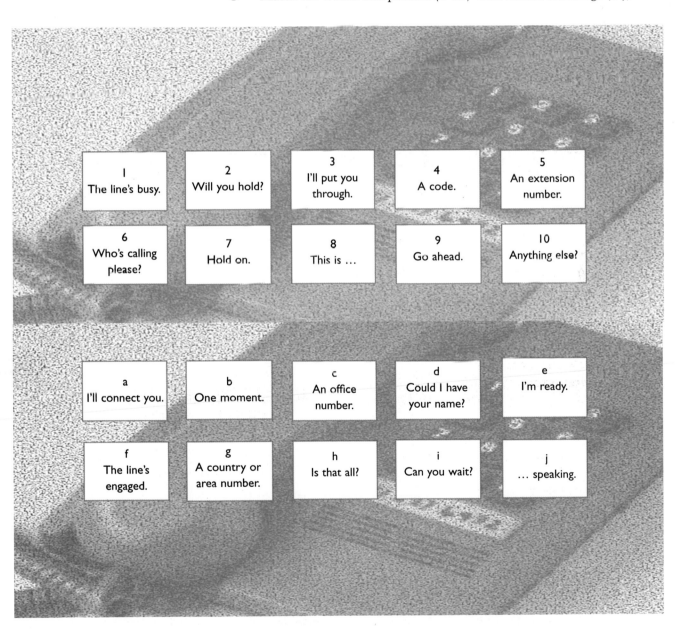

| 1 The line's busy. | 2 Will you hold? | 3 I'll put you through. | 4 A code. | 5 An extension number. |

| 6 Who's calling please? | 7 Hold on. | 8 This is … | 9 Go ahead. | 10 Anything else? |

| a I'll connect you. | b One moment. | c An office number. | d Could I have your name? | e I'm ready. |

| f The line's engaged. | g A country or area number. | h Is that all? | i Can you wait? | j … speaking. |

LANGUAGE WORK

Starting calls

Study these phrases for starting calls.

IDENTIFYING WHO IS SPEAKING	SAYING WHO YOU WANT TO SPEAK TO	
This is Paul Henig. Paul Henig speaking. Is that Julia Gardini?	Could I Can I	speak to ... ?
	I'd like to speak to ... Extension 596, please.	

Supply the missing words in these conversations.

1   **Ms Brunet**   Sales Department, good morning.
    Mr Keller   _____ Helena Steiner, please?
    Ms Brunet   Hold on. I'll get her.

2   **Mrs Steiner**   Hello, Sales.
    Mr Keller   _____ Helena Steiner, please.
    Mrs Steiner   _____ .

3   **Switchboard**   Curtis Holdings.
    Mr Keller   _____ 293, please.
    Miss Delmont Accounts Department.
    Mr Keller   _____ Jean Delmont?
    Miss Delmont Yes, _____ . How can I help you, Mr Keller?

[4] Listen to check your answers.

Pronunciation   **I**   [5a] Can you spell English words over the phone? Listen to the English alphabet and look at the chart. All the letters with similar sounds are grouped together.

1 p*a*ge	2 s*ee*	3 t*e*n	4 f*i*ve	5 h*o*me	6 t*oo*	7 *ar*m
A	B	F	I	O	Q	R
H	C	L	Y		U	
J	D	M			W	
K	E	N				
	G	S				
	P	X				
	T					
	V					

Z is pronounced /zed/ in British English and /ziː/ in American English.

2   Study the chart for a moment then close your book and try writing it on your own.

3   [5b]   Listen and write down the words you hear spelt.

1 _____
2 _____
3 _____
4 _____
5 _____

4   Work with a partner. Take it in turns to dictate abbreviations and write them down. One person dictates the abbreviations below, and the other dictates the ones in File 2 on page 158.

IBM	FOB	OPEC	VIP
EU	VDU	EDP	CIF
JAL	AGM	FBI	IT

Do you know what the letters stand for? You can find out in the Glossary on page 178.

Transferring information

1   Notice these different ways of saying telephone and fax numbers.

91430	*nine one four three zero*	*(American English)*
	nine one four three oh	*(British English)*
6687	*six six eight seven*	*(American English)*
	double six eight seven	*(British English)*

Exchange your work and home numbers with a partner.

2   Work with a partner. Take it in turns to dictate telephone numbers and write them down. One person dictates the telephone numbers below, and the other dictates the ones in File 3 on page 158.

29508
47766
966015
01525 372245
03 916 600721

PRONUNCIATION NOTE

In phone and fax numbers, English speakers normally group the numbers in threes, not in twos as is common elsewhere in Europe.

914306 — *nine one four, three oh six* **not** ~~*nine one, four three, oh six*~~

---

3 When you transfer information by phone, try not to leave long silences or pauses. These phrases will help you.

STARTING	Ready?	Go ahead.
CONTINUING	Have you got that?	Got that.
FINISHING	Anything else?	That's all.
CHECKING	Could you read that back to me?	Could I read that back to you?

Work with a partner. Take it in turns to give each other messages and write them down. One person dictates the messages below, and the other dictates the messages in File 4 on page 158.

Phone Paul Carter
tomorrow morning —
(03) 408-441932.

Send 200 pieces,
ref. no. 306/AJ,
to the Siena
Factory.

Fax exhibition dates
to Vera in São Paulo,
00 55 11 223-3181

Deciding what to do

1 Sometimes we meet new situations or problems and we have to say what action we'll take.

A *The line's busy.*
B *I'll call back later.*

A *Could you take a message?*
B *Hold on. I'll get a pencil.*

Decide what to do in these situations.

A *I'm afraid your train is delayed.*
B *I'll take a taxi.*

1 I'm afraid your train is delayed. (taxi)
2 The President is busy just now. (later)
3 We need some more paper. (order)
4 They don't speak English. (translator)
5 This quotation is very high. (another supplier)
6 I have to go to head office tomorrow. (a lift)
7 They want written confirmation of the order. (fax)
8 Mrs Bell just fainted. (water)

2 Sometimes the person we phone is not available. Match these reasons to the right picture.

a I'm afraid she's on the other line.
b I'm afraid she's off sick.
c I'm afraid she's tied up at the moment.
d I'm afraid he's in a meeting.
e I'm afraid he's not here just now.

Can you think of any more reasons?

3 Work with a partner. Make up conversations deciding what to do when someone is not available.

A *Could I speak to Barbara Morey, please?*
B *I'm afraid she's on holiday this week.*
A *Can you ask her to ring me next week?*

These phrases will help you.

> I'll hold.
> I'll call back later.
> Could you | take a message?
> | give her a message?
> Can you put me through to her secretary?

Requests   **1**   We use these phrases to ask other people to do things.

> Can you ... ?   Could you ... ?   Would you ... ?

You're on the phone. What do you say in these situations?

a   You can't hear the other person.
b   You want them to repeat something.
c   They are speaking too fast.
d   You want them to spell a word.
e   You want them to transfer you to the Finance Department.

2   We can reply to requests like this.

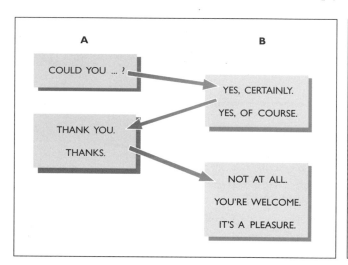

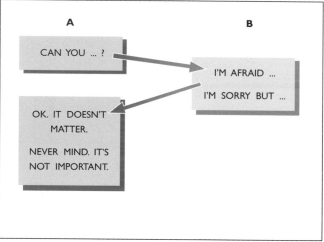

Practise these expressions with a colleague. Ask them to:

a   spell their surname for you.
b   tell you the time.
c   tell you their computer password.
d   give you a lift home tonight.
e   lend you their dictionary.
f   lend you some money.

VOCABULARY NOTE

Put *lend* or *borrow* in these questions.
Could I .... some money?
Could you .... me some money?

Notice we lend **to** someone and we borrow **from** someone. So when we lend, we give; and when we borrow, we take.

3   We use these phrases to ask if it's OK to do things.

ASKING	SAYING YES	SAYING NO
Can I ... ? Could I ... ? May I ... ?	Yes, please do. Of course. * Yeah, go ahead. ** Help yourself.	I'm afraid ... I'm sorry but ...

*Informal   **Inviting someone to take something

Practise with a colleague. You are in their office and you want to:

1   use their phone
2   smoke
3   look at their copy of the production plan
4   copy a file on their computer
5   borrow their copy of the *Economist*
6   borrow their car.

4   Who makes these requests: a customer (C) or supplier (S)?

1   ☐   Can I place an order?
2   ☐   May I have your name and company name?
3   ☐   Could you tell me the delivery address?
4   ☐   Can you deliver next Friday?
5   ☐   Could I have an address for the invoice?
6   ☐   Could you tell me how much it will cost?
7   ☐   May I have a discount?
8   ☐   Would you confirm this order in writing?

Work with a partner. Make up a conversation between a customer and a supplier. Use as many requests as you can.

5   Work in pairs. One person looks at the information below and the other looks at the information in File 6 on page 158.

You sell computers. A foreign customer phones you. Answer their enquiries about your lap-top computer, the NC-200. They will ask about

• your prices
• delivery times
• the guarantee
• discounts
• your terms of payment.

Invent your answers. You can agree to or refuse their requests. Don't forget to write down their details.

SKILLS WORK

Listening

1   ⌷6a⌷   Listen to a message on a telephone answering machine and answer these questions.

   a   Where is Anne Parker going?
   b   How can you reach her?

2   ⌷6b⌷   One of Anne's colleagues listened to Anne's messages and made notes. Listen to the call, find the mistakes in the note below, and correct them.

A MESSAGE FOR: *Anne Parker*

FROM: *Jerry*   ON TEL. NO.:   *01223 50621*

Can't make Tuesday meeting
please call him tomorrow
to fix another time.

☐ PLEASE CALL BACK
☐ WILL CALL AGAIN
☐ URGENT

3   ⌷6c⌷   Now listen to another caller and complete this message.

A MESSAGE FOR: *Anne Parker*

FROM: ON TEL. NO.:

☐ PLEASE CALL BACK
☐ WILL CALL AGAIN
☐ URGENT

4   ⌷6d⌷   Listen to a different recorded message.
Who is it for and what is their extension number?

5   ⌷6e⌷   Listen to some more voice mail instructions. What number do you need to press to:

   a   replay a message?
   b   continue recording a message?
   c   delete a message?
   d   speak to an operator?
   e   transfer out of the voice mail system?

Speaking   Sit back to back with a partner and act out these telephone calls. One person looks at the information below. The other uses the information in File 8 on page 159.

Call 1
Your company's new price lists are still at the printers. You expect them to arrive today. A customer calls with a request. Write down the details.

Call 2
Phone your partner and ask them to speak at the GMB Congress at Queen Margaret's Hall, Manchester on July 13th. You want them to give a talk on their company's current projects.

Writing   **I**   We often write letters to confirm phone calls. Most business letters and faxes contain a lot of standard phrases. Notice how some standard phrases are used in this letter.

FOTOTECHNIQUE

31, rue de Constantine   16102 Cognac Cédex
Téléfax: 45 39 16 11   Télex: 790 962 F   Tél: 45 39 29 24

Mary Thatcher
Sales Manager
Galaxy Computer Supplies
221 Hills Road
Cambridge CB2 2RW

27 October 19xx

START —————— Dear Ms Thatcher,   REFERENCE

With reference to our telephone conversation today,
I am writing to confirm our order for: —————————————   REASON FOR WRITING
10 x Photoconductors Ref. No. 76905 A/K.

REQUEST ————— I would be grateful if you could deliver them as soon as possible.

Thank you for your help. ——————————————————   CLOSING REMARKS

FINISH —————— Yours sincerely,

Christophe Terrien

Christophe Terrien
Director — Procurement.

2 Use this list of standard phrases to complete the letters opposite.

THE START		
Dear Sir or Madam,	*	
Dear	Mr Sloan,	**
	Mrs Sloan,	**
	Miss Sloan,	**
	Ms Sloan,	**
Dear Mary-Lynn,	***	

THE FINISH	
Yours faithfully,	*
Yours sincerely,	**
Best wishes,	***

AMERICAN ENGLISH
Sincerely yours,
Yours truly,

*   suitable if you don't know the name of the person you are writing to.

**   suitable if you know their name.

***   suitable if the person is a close business contact or friend.

THE REFERENCE	
With reference to	your advertisement in the Reporter, ...
	your letter of 25th April, ...
	your phone call today, ...

THE REASON FOR WRITING	
I am writing to	enquire about ...
	apologize for ...
	confirm ...

REQUESTING
Could you possibly ... ?
I would be grateful if you could ...

AGREEING TO REQUESTS
I would be delighted to ...

GIVING BAD NEWS
Unfortunately ...
I'm afraid that ...

ENCLOSING DOCUMENTS
I am enclosing ...
Please find enclosed ...

Close letters with a friendly phrase or reference to future contact.

CLOSING REMARKS	
Thank you for your help.	
Please contact us again if	we can help in any way.
	there are any problems.
	you have any questions.

REFERENCE TO FUTURE CONTACT	
I look forward to	hearing from you soon.
	meeting you next Tuesday.
	seeing you next week.

GEO ORT LTD

COMMERCE WAY LEIGHTON BUZZARD BEDFORDHSIRE LU7 3BW
Tel: 01525 72245 Fax: 01525 72611

Dear Mr Cochet,

REFERENCE ————— ....[1] your phone call today,

....[2] for not sending you our price ————— REASON FOR WRITING

list. ....[3] ,it is still at the

GIVING BAD ————— printers.
NEWS

However, ...[4] a copy of the old ————— ENCLOSING DOCUMENTS

list with the new prices pencilled in.

.....................................[5] ————— CLOSING REMARKS

FINISH ————— ....,[6]

Jacqueline Scott

Jacqueline Scott

GEO ORT LTD

COMMERCE WAY LEIGHTON BUZZARD BEDFORDHSIRE LU7 3BW
Tel: 01525 72245 Fax: 01525 72611

Dear Mary,

REFERENCE ————— ....[1] your phone call yesterday.

.....................................[2] to confirm that ————— REASON FOR WRITING

.....................................[3] come and speak at the GMB

Congress in Manchester on July 13th. ————— AGREEING TO A REQUEST

REQUEST ————— ....[4] send me a map showing how

to get to Queen Mary's Hall?

.....................................[5] ————— REFERENCE TO FUTURE CONTACT

FINISH ————— ....,[6]

Jacky

Jacqueline Scott

OBJECTIVE

to discuss the business activities of companies

TASKS

to describe current projects

•

to exchange numerical information

•

to ask and answer questions about facilities

•

to give a presentation of your company

PRESENTATION

1   What products or services do these companies provide? Do you know anything about their activities?

2   ⎘ Listen to three people talking about these companies. Which company are they talking about?

3   ⎘ Listen to the first speaker again. Make notes on the company.

Employees:	....
Subsidiaries:	....
Turnover:	....
Location of parent company:	....
Number of products:	....
Joint venture partner:	....

PHILIPS

IBM

4 Listen to the second speaker again. Complete these notes.

> * 30,000,000 _____ a year.
> * Fly to 41 _____ in 25 _____ _____.
> * Domestic service has 48 _____ and serves 20 _____.
> * _____ is their number one priority.
> * Currently _____ FANS in their aircraft.
> * FANS are _____ communications and _____ air traffic congestion.

5 Listen to the third speaker again and answer these questions.
1 What's the company's turnover?
2 How many employees are there?
3 What's happening in the company at the moment?

LANGUAGE WORK

Company profiles

Look at these two different ways of asking and answering questions with the verb *have*.

A *How many employees has Philips got?*
B *It's got 250,000.*
A *Has it got any factories in Slovenia?*
B *No, it hasn't.*

A *How many subsidiaries does Philips have?*
B *It has over 120.*
A *Does it have a subsidiary in the UK?*
B *Yes, it does.*

Work with a partner. Ask and answer questions about these companies. (For help with the pronunciation of numbers, see page 175.)

Aussedat Rey Group (paper)
9 industrial sites in France and 1 in Spain.
1 distribution company in France and 1 in Holland.
7 European sales subsidiaries.
1 wood supply subsidiary.

ABB (electrical engineering)
206,000 employees.
1300 companies.
Over 5,000 profit centres.
11 joint ventures in China.

ANA (airline)
123 aircraft in the fleet.
119 scheduled routes.
163 affiliates and subsidiaries.
41 hotels with 12 overseas.

Pirelli (tyres and cables)
2 core businesses: tyres and cables.
78 factories.
Over 41,000 employees.
2,000 research and development specialists.

Carlsberg A/S (beer)
2 major brands: *Carlsberg and Tuborg.*
60 production sites.
Around 100 subsidiaries and associated companies.
80 laboratories at the Carlsberg Research Centre.

Facilities   **1** Would you like an office like this? Why/Why not?

2 Make sentences about the office. Begin:

It's …   *It isn't …*
There's a …   *There isn't a …*
There are some …   *There aren't any …*

Use words from the box.

| computers | plants | coffee machine | small | dark | map |
| photographs | bookcase | very tidy | windows | water fountain |
| similar to my office |

What else can you see in the picture? Make some more sentences.

> **GRAMMAR NOTE**
>
> We use *there is* and *there are* to say things exist or don't exist.
> *There's a child's picture but there aren't any plants.*
>
> We use *it* for things.
> *The picture is on the notice board. It's orange.*
>
> So we often use *there* when we talk about something for the first
> time and *it* when we describe the details.
> *There's a water fountain by the wall. It's two thirds full.*

3 Find out about a partner's place of work. Ask questions about the building and its facilities. Use the words below and begin:

Is the building ... ?　　*Is there a(n) ... ?*　　*Are there any ... ?*

1	modern	8	separate rooms for smokers
2	staff restaurant	9	large car park
3	facilities for disabled staff	10	near a railway station
4	lifts	11	bus stops nearby
5	noisy	12	crèche
6	air conditioning system	13	sport or recreational facilities
7	cold in winter	14	nice to work in

Organizations

Study this organization. Which department:

a puts the products in boxes and crates?
b places ads in magazines?
c pays the staff?
d purchases supplies?
e sells the products to customers?
f plans how to sell new products?
g services the machines and equipment?
h arranges courses for the staff?
i recruits new employees?
j manufactures the products?
k invoices customers?
l looks after customers' problems and complaints?
m dispatches the products and sends them to customers?
n organizes control systems to prevent mistakes?
o deals with taxation, investment, and cash management?

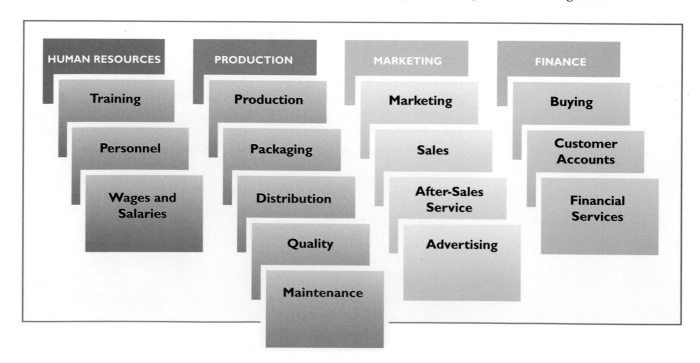

Pronunciation

1 ☐8a There are three ways to pronounce *s* at the end of words: /s/, /z/, and /ɪz/. Practise saying these words.

	SINGULAR	PLURAL
/s/	mistake	mistakes
	product	products
/z/	employee	employees
	sale	sales
/ɪz/	box	boxes
	package	packages

2 ☐8b Now listen to some verbs. They all end with s. Which ones end with an /ɪz/ sound? Tick (✔) them.

1	puts	6	plans	11	invoices
2	places ✔	7	services	12	looks after
3	pays	8	arranges	13	dispatches
4	purchases	9	recruits	14	organizes
5	sells	10	manufactures	15	deals with

Current activities

1 We use the Present Continuous tense to talk about actions that are going on at the moment. Complete these sentences using words from the box.

wait	call	go	build	~~expand~~	develop	stay
get	spend					

a Philips *are expanding* their activities in China.
b Our research department _____ _____ a new drug.
c They _____ _____ at the Dorchester Hotel.
d Someone _____ _____ for you in your office.
e We _____ _____ a new factory in Barcelona.
f I _____ _____ about order no. AJ/2496.
g These products _____ _____ near the end of their life cycle.
h The dollar _____ _____ up.
i The IT department _____ _____ a lot of money on new equipment at the moment.

GRAMMAR NOTE

We use the Present Simple tense to talk about regular activities.
The maintenance department services the equipment.

But we use the Present Continuous tense to talk about temporary activities.
The IT department is spending a lot of money at the moment.

For more information on these two tenses, see the Grammar and Usage Notes, pages 166–167.

---

2 Work with a partner. Find out what's happening in their company at the moment.

- Are they entering any new markets? (Which ones?)
- Are they developing any new products or services? (What?)
- Are they building any new facilities? (What? Where?)
- Are they working in any joint ventures? (What?)

And what's happening in their department or division?
- Are they taking on new staff? (Why?)
- Are they reorganizing any work systems? (Which ones? Why?)
- Are they introducing a quality programme? (What exactly?)
- Are they introducing new technology? (What?)

Company strengths

1 Are these statements true for your company?

We produce high quality products.
We provide a high quality service.
We use the most advanced technology.
We are in close contact with the market.
We produce a wide range of products.
We invest a lot of money in research and development.
We have sales representatives all over the world.
We are market leaders.

Why is your company special? What is your company's main strength?

2 What do you know about McDonald's? Are these facts true or false? What do you think?

	T	F
a Three new McDonald's stores open every day.	☐	☐
b McDonald's charge high prices.	☐	☐
c McDonald's spend more on advertising than anyone else.	☐	☐
d There is a Hamburger University.	☐	☐
e The company CEO has a computer in his office.	☐	☐
f McDonald's prefer American managers to run overseas stores.	☐	☐

Now read this article and find out.

SERVICE WITH A SMILE

Three new McDonald's stores open somewhere in the world each day. There are now over 14,000 McDonald's stores worldwide and sales are over $23 billion. So how do they do it? What are the company's strengths?

VALUE
McDonald's keep prices low. They concentrate on increasing market share.

ADVERTISING
McDonald's spend $1.4 billion annually on marketing, more than any other company in the world.

TRAINING
Every employee receives at least two or three days' training and all managers attend regular courses. The company even has its own Hamburger University in Oakbrook, Illinois.

FACE-TO-FACE MEETINGS
The company headquarters don't have an e-mail system and there's no computer in the CEO's office but ideas still fly around. There are regular meetings between people in the same region and people in the same line of work.

CLOSE RELATIONSHIPS WITH SUPPLIERS
McDonald's work closely with their suppliers to make sure they can meet the McDonald's specifications.

CULTURAL SENSITIVITY
Before they enter a new country's market, they research the culture thoroughly. And they employ local staff if they can.

CUSTOMER SERVICE
The restaurants are clean, the service is quick and every McDonald's burger comes with a smile.

3 Interview a partner about their company. Ask:

a Are your prices low or high compared with your competitors?
b Is advertising important to your business?
c What training do your staff receive?
d Do you hold regular meetings with your colleagues and counterparts?
e Do you have close relationships with your suppliers?
f Are your managers locals or foreigners?
g Why do your customers like your products/service?

SKILLS WORK

Listening   9   A manager from BICC describes her company. Listen and complete the organization chart below.

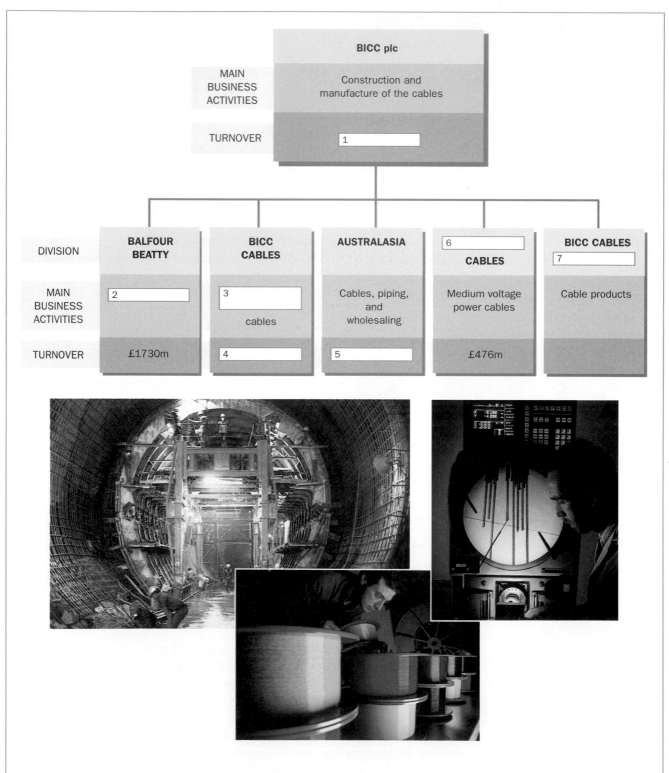

	BICC plc			
MAIN BUSINESS ACTIVITIES	Construction and manufacture of the cables			
TURNOVER	1			

DIVISION	BALFOUR BEATTY	BICC CABLES	AUSTRALASIA	6 _____ CABLES	BICC CABLES 7 _____
MAIN BUSINESS ACTIVITIES	2	3 _____ cables	Cables, piping, and wholesaling	Medium voltage power cables	Cable products
TURNOVER	£1730m	4	5	£476m	

Speaking **1** Prepare to make a short presentation about a company to the class. You can talk about your own company or one of the companies from this unit. Write notes first. Don't write sentences – just write key words and numbers. (Guess any information you don't know.)

	MY COMPANY	THE GROUP
Products/Services		
Main customers		
Locations (factories, branches, etc.)		
Size (no. of employees/turnover)		
Main strength		
Current projects		
Other information?		

2 Now decide on the structure of your presentation. These phrases will help you order the information.

THE INTRODUCTION	ORDERING INFORMATION
I'd like to tell you about …	I'll begin with … Now I'll move on to … turn to …

CHECKING UNDERSTANDING	FINISHING
Is that clear? Are you with me? OK so far?	Are there any questions? Thank you very much.

Use your notes to give the presentation and answer questions from your colleagues.

OBJECTIVE

to exchange
information about
products and services

TASKS

to give effective
descriptions and
explanations

•

to exchange
information on size
and dimension

•

to make enquiries
about transporting a
product

•

to evaluate different
ways of recording new
words

•

to make an informal
product presentation

PRESENTATION

1   Label these inventions with words from the box.

> a   the aerosol can   b   the pinball machine   c   the bar code
> d   the remote control   e   the ring-pull opener

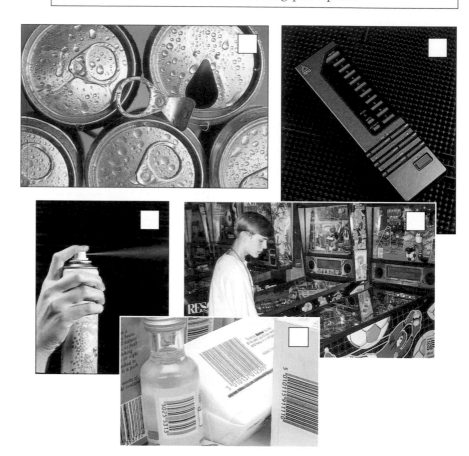

2   🔟   Close your book and listen to some people talking about the different inventions. Which invention are they talking about?

3   🔟ᵃ   Listen to the person talking about the aerosol can again. You can read the text at the same time.

> This was designed in World War II by the United States Department of Agriculture. It was originally developed to protect soldiers from insects. Today's version contains no CFC gases and is designed to be environmentally-friendly. A famous user was James Bond. He uses one to make a flame thrower in the movie *Live and Let Die*.

Why do they say 'was designed' in one place, but 'is designed' in another?

4 [10b] Listen to the person talking about the bar code again and read the text.

> Originally these were circular. They were first used in the early 1960s to identify railroad cars and keep efficient records of stock in warehouses. Now supermarkets use rectangular versions for point-of-sale stocktaking. Some people say they are the sign of the devil. They point out that the two thin lines at both ends and in the centre are a way of representing the number six. So every product in every store contains the numbers 666 in code.

Was is the past form of *is*. What is the past form of *are*? Find it in the text.

5 [10c] Complete this text with *was* or *were*. Then listen to the person talking about the ring-pull again and check your answers.

> These _____¹ invented in 1963 by Ermel Freize, a metals expert, after a family picnic. It _____² a very hot day and there _____³ lots of cold drinks around, but no can opener. Ermel _____⁴ determined to find a solution to the problem. And this is it. It tears a strip of metal from the can and leaves a hole to drink from. There _____⁵ a litter problem with the original pull-off type and there _____⁶ a lot of complaints, but now we use a push-in type.

6 [10d] Listen to the person talking about the pinball machine again and read the text.

> Originally these were designed to entertain the unemployed in Chicago in the Depression years of the 1930s. The first machines weren't very sophisticated and it wasn't a very interesting game to play by modern standards, but it was only a penny a try. A famous user today is Andrew Lloyd Webber, the composer of musicals, such as *Phantom of the Opera* and *Cats*. He uses one to help him relax.

What are the negative forms of *was* and *were*? Find them in the text.

7 [10e] Complete this text with *was*, *were*, *wasn't*, and *weren't*. Then listen to the person talking about the remote control again and check your answers.

> The first version in the 1950s _____¹ remote. It _____² connected to the television by a wire. So there _____³ a wire across the user's living room floor and it _____⁴ very safe. The early models _____⁵ very popular and _____⁶ replaced by ultra sound models in the early 1970s. These _____⁷ fine for humans, but _____⁸ popular with dogs and cats. Today we use infra-red versions to change channels.

Description

LANGUAGE WORK

I Do you know what all these adjectives mean?

cold	old-fashioned	expensive	inefficient
unfriendly	crowded	five-star	busy
wonderful	boring	useless	short
tiring	inexperienced	informative	windy
fast	entertaining	large	uncomfortable

2 *Cold* is the opposite of *hot*.

1 Find opposites for these adjectives in the box.
   slow, cheap, long, small, modern, interesting, terrible.

2 What are the opposites of these adjectives? (Look in the box to check your answers.)
   comfortable, efficient, friendly, experienced, useful

3 Find adjectives in the box to describe the things. Then think of different hotels, journeys, etc. What other adjectives can you use to describe them?

THE WEATHER

A HOTEL

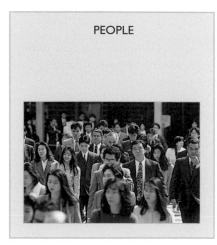

A JOURNEY

ENGLISH LESSONS

PEOPLE

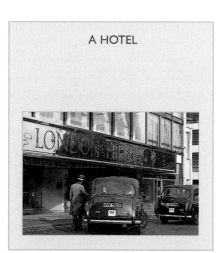

RESTAURANTS

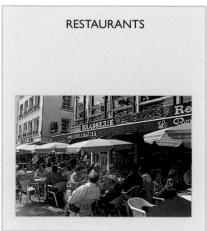

3   Work with a partner.

1   Imagine one of you went on an excellent training course in England. Answer your partner's questions about:
- the journey
- the lectures
- the trainers
- the hotel
- the weather
- English pubs

What was the journey like?
What were the lectures like?

2   Now imagine one of you went on a terrible camping holiday in England. Answer your partner's questions about:
- the journey
- the weather
- the camp sites you stayed at
- the people you met
- the restaurants you visited
- English food

What was the journey like?
What were the camp sites like?

4   *Interesting* and *interested* are both adjectives. *Interesting* describes a quality something has. *Interested* describes a reaction. Complete these sentences with *interesting* and *interested*.

1   It was an _____ meeting.
2   I was very _____.
3   There are a lot of _____ buildings in Rio de Janeiro.
4   That's an _____ idea.
5   We're _____ in your products.

5   Do these adjectives describe the products or services your company sells or provides?

efficient   reliable   good value   sophisticated
technologically advanced   professional   expensive
high-quality   well designed   environmentally-friendly

Think of more adjectives to describe your products or services. Say what is special about them.

Our prices are competitive.
Our staff are well trained.
We offer a wide variety of options.

Explaining what you need

1 Label the photographs using the words in the box.

microphone	projector	remote control	flip-chart	lectern
marker	socket	carousel		

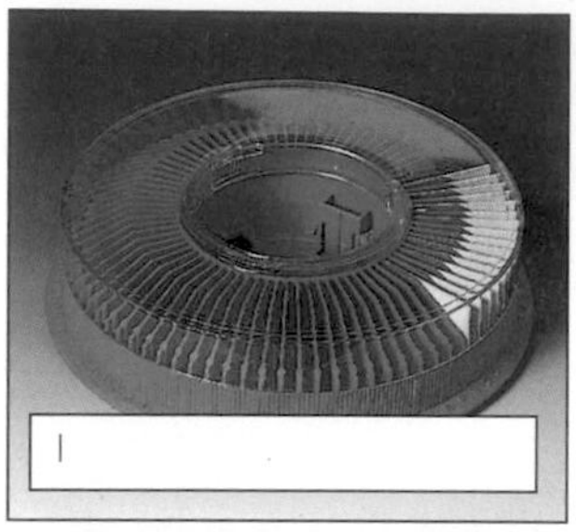

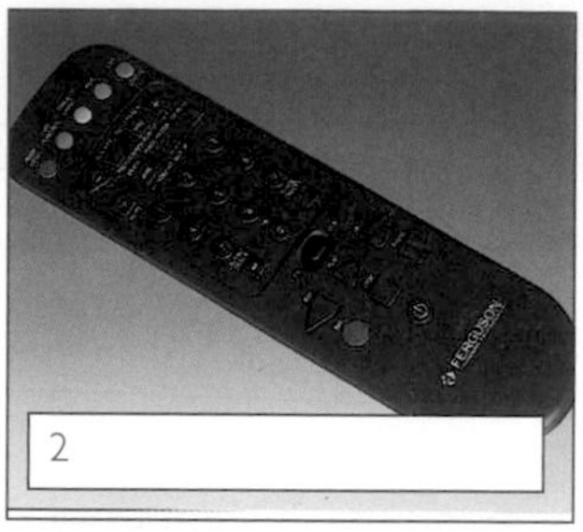

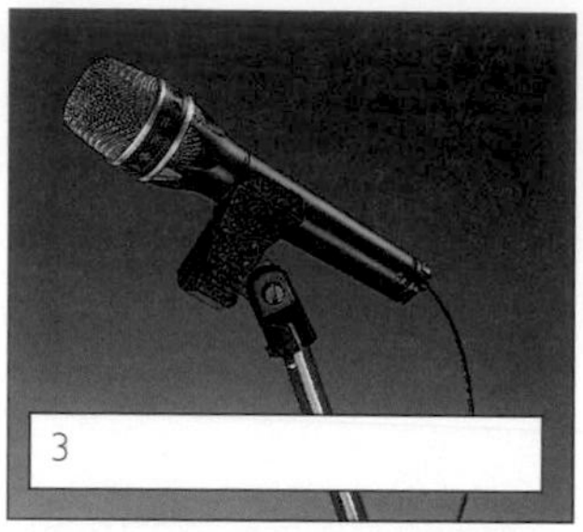

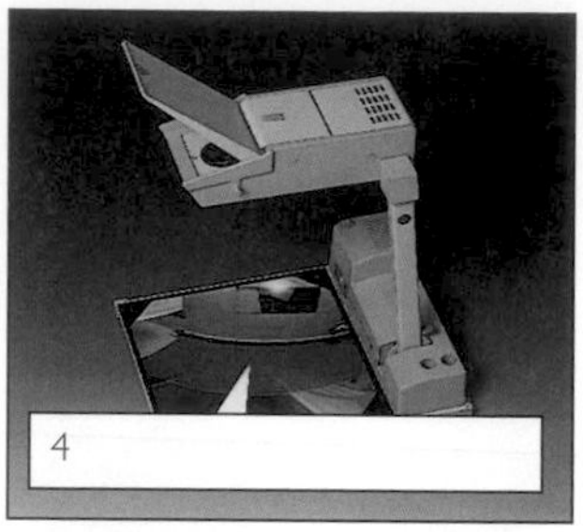

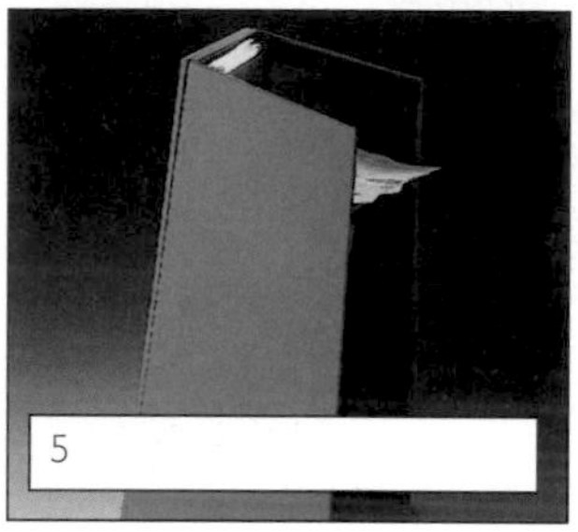

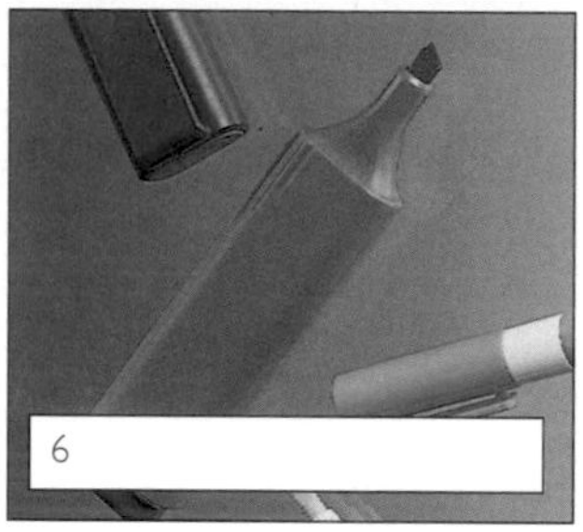

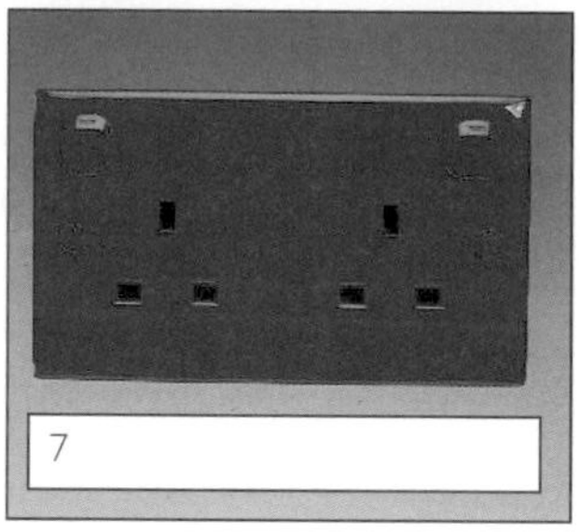

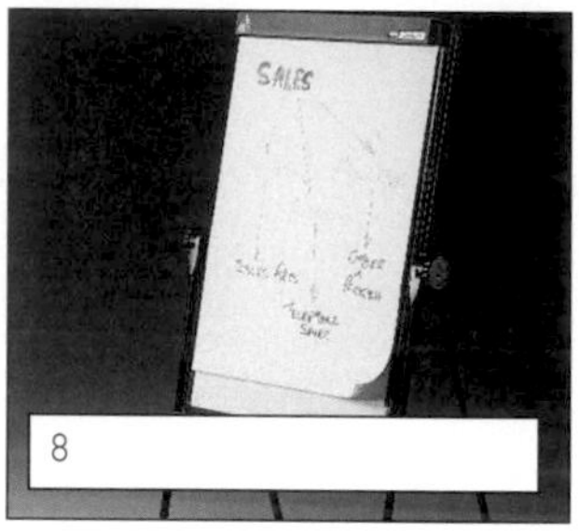

2 [11] Someone is preparing to give a presentation and they can't remember the names of the things they need. Listen and help them.

Presenter I need a thing to show transparencies.
You Do you mean a projector? There's one here.

3 Now choose one of the items (or something else in the room if you like) and describe it to a partner. They must guess what it is.

You *It's similar to a note pad and it's used to write on. It's white, rectangular, and made of paper.*
Partner *You mean a flip-chart.*

Size and dimension

1 Study these ways of describing dimension. Then cover them up, look at the diagram opposite, and try to remember them.

How long is it? How wide is it? How high is it?	It's 484.5cm long. It's 165.0cm wide. It's 157.5cm high.	The length is 484.5cm. The width is 165.0cm. The height is 157.5cm.
How heavy is it? How much does it weigh?	It weighs 2,570 kg. The weight is 2,570 kg.	
How much can it carry? What's the maximum load?	It can carry 1,160 kg. It's 1,160 kg.	

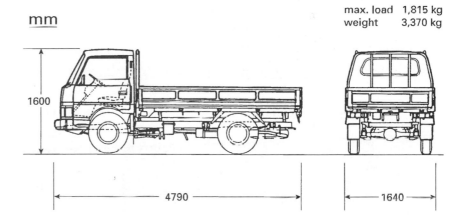

mm

max. load   1,160 kg
weight   2,570 kg

1575

1650   4845

2   A transport manager is thinking of buying some pick-up trucks for his fleet. Act out the conversation with the salesperson. Ask and answer questions about the size and dimension of the truck below.

mm

max. load   1,815 kg
weight   3,370 kg

1600

4790   1640

3   Work with a partner. One person looks at the information below. The other looks at the information in File 7 on page 158.

You want to forward some large steel components to a customer in Rome. Phone your partner's forwarding company and make enquiries.

Your information

The components are in 6 wooden crates.

The dimensions of each crate are: Length – 4m Width – 2m Height – 2.5m

The cubic capacity of each crate is 20m³.

Each crate weighs 1,500 kg.

Information required

How many trailers do you need?

How much does it cost?

How long does it take to drive a trailer to Rome?

Pronunciation

Some English words have the same pronunciation but different meanings and spellings.

/weɪ/   *How much does it **weigh**?*
        *Could you tell me the **way** to the town centre?*
/weɪt/ *The **weight** is 3,370 kg.*
        *I'll **wait** in the car for you.*

12a Listen to some words and write them down. Write different spellings for each word.

1 _____
2 _____
3 _____
4 _____
5 _____
6 _____
7 _____
8 _____
9 _____

Now turn to File 13 on page 160.

Sorting words

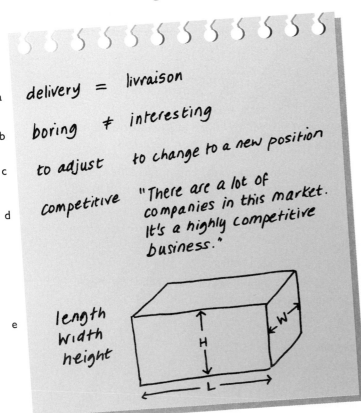

a delivery = livraison

b boring ≠ interesting

c to adjust   to change to a new position

d competitive   "There are a lot of companies in this market. It's a highly competitive business."

e length
   width
   height

1 How do you write down the new English words you want to learn? Have you got a system? Here are some different ways of recording the meaning of a new word. Which one is

- an example sentence?
- a diagram or picture?
- an explanation in English?
- a translation?
- an opposite?

And which are good ways of recording words? Which ones

- are quick and simple?
- explain the meaning clearly?
- help you to use the word in a sentence?
- make the word easy to remember?

2 Record these words in **different** ways. Use a dictionary to help you, if necessary. (What is the best way of recording each one?)

truck, inefficient, component, weight, reliable

3 Sorting words into groups can help you remember them. You can group together words belonging to the same family.

Complete this table:

VERB	NOUN	NOUN (PEOPLE)
to produce	production	producer
	sale	
		advertiser
	management	
to employ		

4 You can group together words that often go together. Think of more words to add to these boxes.

to make	a product
	a presentation
	a mistake
	a phone call
	a ....

to manufacture	a product
to sell	
to market	
to design	
to	

5 You can group together words connected with the same topic. Use the words in the box to complete this network.

length   easy maintenance   sophisticated   dimensions
shape   selling points   domestic   plastic   circular
modern   user-friendly controls   steel

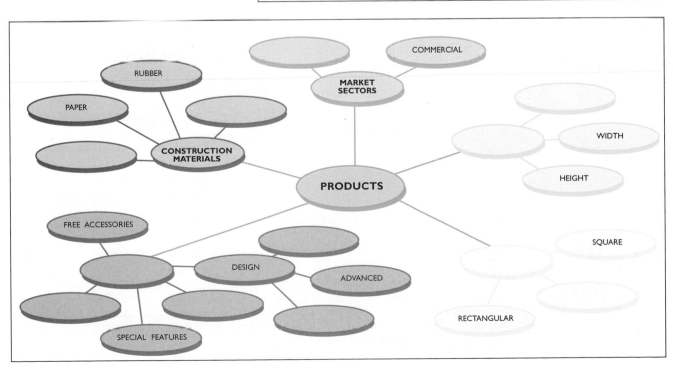

SKILLS WORK

Speaking 1

When you don't have the exact word you need in English, you have to find another way of communicating what you mean, using words you do know. So, for example, when you can't remember the word 'newspaper' you have to paraphrase and say 'the thing you read every day in the morning'. It's important to do this quickly to increase your fluency in the language and this exercise practises this skill.

Work with a partner to complete the crossword. One person uses the crossword below and the other uses the crossword in File 9 on page 159. There are no clues but your partner has the words you need and you have the words they need. You can say anything you like to help your partner, but of course, you can't say the missing word.

What's one down? What's thirteen across?

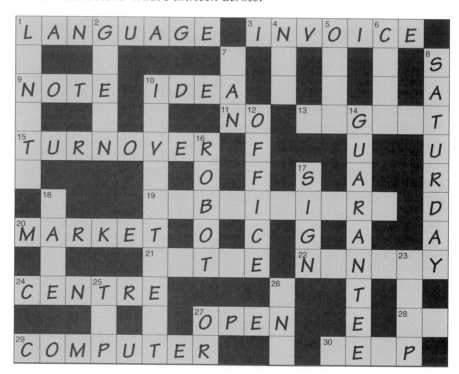

Listening 1

How do you keep fit? Do you use an exercise cycle? Why/Why not? Who buys these machines? What sort of features are they interested in?

2 You are going to hear a sales manager briefing his sales team on this product. Before you listen, label the cycle with the words in the box.

> **a** seat   **b** foot straps   **c** handle bars   **d** handle bar grips
> **e** speed and distance meter

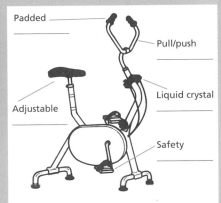

Padded

Pull/push

Liquid crystal

Adjustable

Safety

SPECIFICATIONS
Registered design

LENGTH _____

WIDTH _____

HEIGHT _____

WEIGHT

3 [13] Listen and complete the specifications.

4 [13] Listen again and complete these sentences.

1 The AC4 was very successful _____ .
2 The AC4 is popular with _____ .
3 The AC4 doesn't sell well in _____ .
4 The AC5 is designed for _____ .
5 The AC5 is suitable for _____ .
6 The special feature of the AC5 is that it's _____ .

5 Match the words and phrases with similar meanings.

1 low cost   a strongly made
2 portable   b collapsible
3 high stability   c good value
4 robust construction   d doesn't take up much space
5 compact   e easy to change to a new position
6 adjustable   f easy to pick up and carry about
7 folds up for easy storage   g doesn't fall over easily

Speaking 2

Work in groups of three or four. You are looking for executive toys to give your customers and clients this Christmas and you want to give them something unusual. You have all collected information on a different product. Read the information and then take it in turns to describe your product to the group. Tell them about:

• its use or purpose
• its size and dimensions
• the accessories (extras) it comes with
• the price.

Decide what to buy your customers. Each person in your group needs to look at different information. (See Files: 5 on page 158, 16 on page 160, 24 on page 162, and 30 on page 164.)

OBJECTIVE

to report on past actions

TASKS

to talk about events in a company's history

•

to establish what happened on a business trip

•

to deal with customer complaints

•

to read about product launches and discuss what went wrong

•

to give an account of a project in your workplace

PRESENTATION

I 　[14]　Listen to someone describing the history of a product development project. Number these actions in the order they happened.

☐ modify the designs
☐ run a feasibility study
☐ send the drawings to potential customers
☐ run tests
☐ shelve the project
☐ design and construct the prototype
☐ prepare detailed drawings

2 ⌷14⌷ Listen again and make a note of when these things happened.

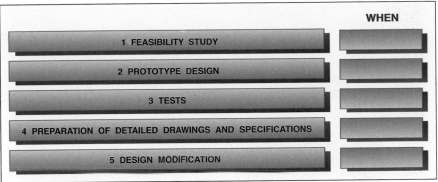

3 What problems did they have

1 at the test stage?
2 at the drawings and specifications stage?
3 at the design modification stage?
4 at the manufacturing stage?

Pronunciation

I Regular verbs end in *-ed* in the Past Simple tense. This is pronounced in three different ways.

/d/ *joined, prepared*
/t/ *finished, discussed*
/ɪd/ *constructed, started*

⌷15a⌷ Listen to a description of a project. Notice how we pronounce the Past Simple tense verbs. Do they end in /d/, /t/ or /ɪd/?

We **prepared** designs and **discussed** them with the clients before we **started**. We **looked** at the drawings together and they **liked** them. We **provided** detailed specifications and **showed** them the plans at every stage. They **discovered** a few small mistakes but we **corrected** them. We **changed** anything they didn't like. We even **included** extra features when they **asked** for them. Then as soon as we **finished** they **complained**. They said they **wanted** something different.

2 ⌷15b⌷ Listen to the verbs again and complete the table.

/d/	/t/	/ɪd/
prepared	discussed	started

Notice that we use the voiced /ɪd/ sound with verbs that end with /d/ or /t/.

Company history
LANGUAGE WORK

THE HISTORY OF THE NISSAN MOTOR COMPANY

1925

Three small motor companies merge to form the Dat Jidosha Seizo Company.

1932

The company produces the first Datsun car.

1934

NISSAN MOTOR CO., LTD.

The owners re-name the company 'The Nissan Motor Company Ltd'.

1935

Nissan opens the Yokohama plant.

1936

Nissan introduces mass production methods.

1938

Nissan stops producing passenger cars and concentrates on truck* manufacture.

* British English: lorry

1947

After World War II, Nissan begins car production again.

1958

A Datsun 210 wins the Australian Rally.

1966

Nissan sets up its first foreign manufacturing operation in Mexico.

1980

The National Space Development Agency of Japan send a rocket into space, with solid-fuel rocket boosters designed and produced by Nissan.

PHOTO BY NASDA

1981

Nissan makes an agreement with Volkswagen to produce the Santana in Japan.

1992, 1993, 1994

In the UK, Nissan earns a Queen's Award for Export Achievement for three years running.

1 Work in pairs. Ask and answer questions about the Nissan Motor Company.

A *What happened in 1925?*
B *Three small motor companies merged.*
A *What happened in 1947?*
B *Nissan began car production again.*

Regular verbs end -*ed* in the Past Simple tense. Irregular verbs have a special form. There is a table of irregular verbs on page 177.

2 Ask and answer more questions about Nissan.

A *When did the original three companies merge?*
B *In 1925.*
A *When did … ?*

For information on Past Simple tense questions, see page 168.

3 Choose the correct verbs from the boxes to complete the passage. Remember to use the Past Simple tense.

| be | sell | ~~establish~~ |
| grow | import | have |

| find | decide | begin |
| become | | |

| achieve | be able to | |
| have to | supply | |

| be | be | win | set up |
| launch | start | | |

THE HISTORY OF NISSAN IN THE UK

Nissan *established* a small trading company in 1969. It
_____¹ cars from Japan and _____² them in the UK. The
company only _____³ 0.2% of the market in 1970 but it
_____⁴ fast. By 1974 it _____⁵ the UK's leading car
importer.

When the UK _____⁶ a major export market, Nissan
_____⁷ to build an assembly plant. After a long search it
_____⁸ a suitable site in Tyne and Wear. Cars _____⁹
rolling off the production line in 1986.

At first, the plant _____¹⁰ limit production because of the
JAMA import restriction agreement. But by 1988 UK companies
_____¹¹ the majority of components and Nissan _____¹²
the target of 60% local content. The plant _____¹³ increase
production.

In 1991 Nissan _____¹⁴ a new distribution company and it
_____¹⁵ operations in January 1992 with a network of 150
dealers. By the end of the year there _____¹⁶ 267. Nissan
_____¹⁷ the Micra (March) in 1993 and it _____¹⁸ the
European Car of the Year Award. It _____¹⁹ the first
Japanese- badged car ever to win.

4 Work in pairs. One person uses the information below and the other uses the information in File 15 on page 160.

You are a newspaper reporter writing an article on Facit, a Swedish office equipment company. Ask the public relations officer for information to complete these notes.
When did Facit start trading?
What happened in 1889?

FACIT

_____	Facit started trading in Sweden as a small copper mining company.
1889	_____
_____	Facit established its first subsidiary in Denmark.
1938	_____
_____	Facit introduced its products into the USA.
_____	Facit established subsidiaries in the USA and Brazil.
1956	_____
_____	The Facit 2254 calculator became standard in Tokyo's largest bank.
1985	_____
1990	Facit opened a marketing co-ordination centre in Brussels.
1994	_____

Facit started trading in the fifteenth century as a mining company.

Facit produced wooden furniture for many years.

Facit began manufacturing mechanical calculators in 1924.

Typewriters were added to the range when Facit purchased Halda Typewriters.

Today, Facit is a leading trading and distribution company within the office and computer industry. The product range includes calculators, printers, display terminals, and portable electronic devices.

Saying when

I Study the different prepositions we use with these times.

IN	ON	AT
1999	Saturday	5.30
August	2 May	Easter
winter		the end of the war
the afternoon		

Which preposition do we use with:

1 dates?
2 months?
3 days of the week?
4 years?
5 seasons?

6 religious festivals?
7 hours of the clock?
8 parts of the day?
9 points in time?

2 Put the right preposition with these times.

1 ____ 1969
2 ____ Thursday
3 ____ 19 January
4 ____ January
5 ____ midnight
6 ____ the morning

7 ____ Christmas
8 ____ Christmas Day
9 ____ the autumn (*US*: the fall)
10 ____ the 1960s
11 ____ the weekend
12 ____ the turn of the century

3 Ask a colleague when they did these things. Make sure they use a preposition in their answer.

When did you join your company?
In 1981.

1 joined their company
2 got married
3 got up this morning
4 last had a holiday
5 bought their car

6 last spoke to someone in English
7 last gave someone a present
8 last had a beer

Reporting on a trip

I Find out about your partner's last business trip. First write some questions.

Town/country	Where .... ?
Method of transport	.... travel?
Journey time	How long .... ?
Accommodation	Where .... ?
Length of stay	.... stay?
Purpose of trip	Why .... ?
Opinion of trip	Was ....successful?

2 Now practise asking the questions with a partner. (The person answering them can tell the truth or invent answers.)

Complaints

1 ⌷16a⌷ Listen to half of a telephone call. What is it about?

Flora	Hello Roger. It's Flora Silveira.
Roger	_____
Flora	I'm fine, thanks. And you?
Roger	_____
Flora	I'm afraid there's a problem with our order. You delivered the wrong quantity.
Roger	_____
Flora	60. We asked for 80.
Roger	_____
Flora	Thanks a lot. Can you send them today?
Roger	_____
Flora	No, that's all thanks.

What is Roger saying? Can you guess? Write in the words.

2 ⌷16b⌷ Now listen to the whole call and check your answers. Then turn to File 20 on page 161.

3 When customers make complaints, it's important to ask questions to get all the facts you need. Ask questions about these problems.

A *You delivered the wrong quantity.*
B *Oh dear. What quantity did we deliver?*
A *300. We ordered 3,000.*
B *I'm sorry about that.*

1 You delivered the wrong quantity.
   (300. We ordered 3,000.)
2 You sent the order to the wrong address.
   (30 South Road. We're at 40.)
3 You invoiced us for the wrong amount.
   (£4,000 instead of $4,000.)
4 The goods came with the wrong accessories.
   (Plastic hooks. We wanted metal.)
5 The cover was the wrong colour.
   (Black. We asked for brown.)
6 The handles were the wrong size.
   (15cm. We ordered 10cm.)
7 The goods arrived on the wrong day.
   (Friday. We asked for Tuesday.)
8 The case was no good.
   (The glass was broken.)

4 What possible reasons are there for these problems?
We're very short staffed at the moment.
Our computer crashed and we lost a lot of data.

Think of some more excuses.

5 Here are some useful phrases for dealing with complaints. Complete the chart with phrases from the box.

> a I'll find out what happened and let you know.
> b I'm afraid we're not responsible for damage in transit.
> c Would you like a refund?
> d I'll look into it straight away.
> e Would you like us to repair it?
> f We're very sorry about this but it's not our fault.

DEALING WITH COMPLAINTS
MAKING OFFERS
Would you like a replacement?
PROMISING ACTION
We'll send the rest immediately.
REFUSING RESPONSIBILITY
We reserve the right to make small changes to products.

Can you think of any more phrases to add to the chart?

6 Work with a partner. Act out the complaints in Exercise 3 again. Deal with them. Make up excuses and/or use phrases from the chart.

7 Discuss these questions with a partner.

1 What sort of complaints do you have to deal with?
2 What advice would you give to someone who has to deal with complaints?

SKILLS WORK

Reading | Sometimes products don't sell well in a new market. Suggest what went wrong in these cases.

WHAT WENT WRONG?

1 Western companies had problems selling refrigerators in Japan until they changed the design to make them quieter.

2 In Saudi Arabia, newspaper adverts for an airline showed an attractive hostess serving champagne to happy passengers. A lot of passengers cancelled their flight reservations.

3 An airline company called itself Emu, after the Australian bird. But Australians didn't want to use the airline.

4 A TV commercial for a cleaning product showed a little girl cleaning up the mess her brother made. The commercial caused problems in Canada.

5 Several European and American firms couldn't sell their products in Dubai when they ran their advertising campaign in Arabic.

6 A soap powder ad had a picture of dirty clothes on the left, a box of soap in the middle and clean clothes on the right. The soap didn't sell well in the Middle East.

7 A company had problems when it tried to introduce instant coffee to the French market.

8 A toothpaste manufacturer couldn't sell its product in parts of South-East Asia.

9 An American golf ball manufacturer launched its products in Japan packed in boxes of four. It had to change the pack size.

10 A ladies' electric shaver sold well throughout Europe, but not in Italy.

2   Here are the reasons for the problems, but they are in the wrong order. Number them from 1 to 10. How many did you get right?

☐   In Japanese the word for *four* sounds like the word for *death*. Things don't sell well packed in fours.

☐   People thought the commercial was too sexist and reinforced old male/female stereotypes.

☐   Unveiled women don't mix with men in Saudi Arabia and alcohol is illegal.

☐   90% of the population came from Pakistan, India, Iran and elsewhere, so Arabic was the wrong language.

☐   It seems Italian men prefer ladies' legs unshaven.

☐   The advertisers forgot that in that part of the world people usually read from right to left.

☐   The people in this area didn't want white teeth. They thought darkly-stained teeth were beautiful and they tried to blacken them.

☐   Japanese homes were small and sometimes walls were made of paper. It was important for the refrigerators to be quiet.

☐   Making 'real' coffee was an important part of the French way of life. Instant coffee was too casual.

☐   The emu can't fly.

3   Look through the passages again and find the words below.
1   Two abbreviations for the word *advertisement*
2   The word for people who advertise
3   The word for an advertisement on television

Speaking   Think of a project you took part in at work, for example:
• the launch of a new product/service
• a product development project
• the design/introduction of a new system
• a construction project
• setting up a new venture/operation

1   What were the objectives or goals of the project?
2   List the tasks you performed to achieve those objectives.
3   How long did each task take? How long did it take to complete the project?
4   What were your main problems?
5   What were the results of the project?

Work in small groups. Take it in turns to explain your projects to the group and answer questions.

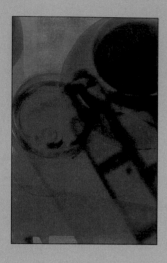

OBJECTIVE

to hold social
conversations with
business contacts

TASKS

to welcome an
overseas visitor
•
to order food at a
business lunch
•
to make, accept, and
refuse offers
•
to discuss leisure
interests
•
to read and discuss an
article on executive life
styles

PRESENTATION

I   In the office

1   ☐17a☐ Kevin Donoghue is welcoming a client, Paolo Farneti, to his
office. Listen to the conversation. Are these statements true or false?

		T	F
a	This is their first meeting.	☐	☐
b	Kevin gave Paolo directions.	☐	☐
c	The journey took two hours.	☐	☐
d	Paolo wants white coffee.	☐	☐

2   Act out their conversation with a partner. The pictures below will
help you remember it.

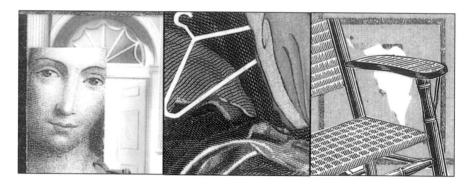

2   In the car

1   [17b] Kevin is driving Paolo to a restaurant. Listen to the
conversation. Are these statements true or false?

		T	F
a	This is Paolo's first visit to Cambridge.	☐	☐
b	Kevin offers to show Paolo round next week.	☐	☐
c	Kevin plays golf.	☐	☐
d	Paolo goes skiing once a month in winter.	☐	☐

2   Imagine you're welcoming a visitor to your home town. Act out a
similar conversation. Complete this dialogue first.

A   Is this your first visit to _____ [1] ?
B   Yes, _____ [2]. I'd love to see _____ [3] .
A   Then let me show you round tomorrow after the meeting.
B   That's very kind _____ [4] . Is there a good _____ [5] here?
A   Yes, there is. _____ [6] interested in sport?
B   Yes. I play _____ [7] and I go _____ [8] . What about you?
A   I _____ [9] .

3   In the restaurant

Kevin and Paolo are ordering wine in a restaurant. Before you listen,
read the conversation below and guess the missing words. Use one
word per space.

Waiter   The wine list, sir.
Kevin   Thank you. Let's see. What _____ [1] of wine do you
like, Paolo?
Paolo   I _____ [2] white.
Kevin   _____ [3] or dry?
Paolo   Dry.
Kevin   Then let's have the Chablis. It's usually very good.
Paolo   How _____ [4] do you come here?
Kevin   About once a month. (to the waiter) Excuse me.
Waiter   Yes, sir?
Kevin   We'll _____ [5] the Chablis, please. Number 63.
Paolo   And I'd _____ [6] a bottle of mineral water too, please.

[17c] Listen to the conversation and check your answers.

LANGUAGE WORK

Business lunches | Match the dishes on the menu to the pictures.

STARTERS

Smoked Salmon
Slices of best Scottish salmon served with brown bread and butter

Cheese Tart
Light crisp pastry with a creamy cheese filling

Garden Soup
A delicate summer vegetable soup with herbs

MAIN COURSES

Duck with Green Peas
Duck stewed with spices, herbs and freshly picked peas

Dover Sole
Poached and served in a cream sauce with prawns and asparagus tips

Roast Leg of Welsh Lamb
Flavoured with garlic and rosemary, and served with onion sauce

PUDDINGS

Summer Pudding
A classic combination of summer fruits (cherries, raspberries, black and redcurrants) and bread

Strawberries and Cream
Our own fresh English strawberries

Chocolate Fudge Cake
A rich, sticky chocolate cake

CHEESE

A wide selection of English cheeses

Liqueurs
Coffee

1 	2 	3 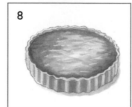	4 	5 
6 	7 	8 	9 	10 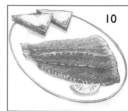

2 Put these different foods into the right list.

peas	lamb	pork	sole	salmon	duck	raspberries
chicken	cauliflower	strawberries		beef	cherries	

meat	fish	poultry	vegetables	fruit

Think of more words to add to each list. What is your favourite meal?

3 Work in small groups. Appoint someone as the waiter/waitress and give them your orders.

I'll have the cheese tart.
Salmon for me. What about you, John?
I'd like the duck.
Garden soup please, and I'd like Dover Sole to follow.
What do you suggest?

Offers

1 Look at the words in **bold type** in these sentences.

Would you like a biscuit?   (*a* + single countable noun)
Would you like some wine?   (*some* + uncountable noun)
Would you like some grapes?   (*some* + plural countable noun)

Take it in turns to offer food and drink.

OFFERING		SAYING YES	SAYING NO
Would you like	a ... ? some ... ?	Thanks. Yes please. I'd love one. some.	No, thanks. It looks lovely, but ...

2   You can make uncountable nouns countable by using *a ... of ...* .

wine – a glass of wine   *bread – a piece of bread*

Find the uncountable nouns in the pictures on page 61. Make them countable. Use phrases like *some cake* or *a piece of cake*.

Pronunciation

[18] Listen to this conversation, then practise reading it with a partner.

Customer	I'd like a cheese sandwich, a chicken sandwich, and a cherry tart served with chocolate sauce.
Waiter	OK. So that's a cheese sandwich, a chicken sandwich, and a cherry tart served with chocolate sauce.
Customer	Ah, sorry. Can I change the cherry tart served with chocolate sauce?
Waiter	Certainly.
Customer	I'll have fresh English strawberries served with sugar and sweet champagne.
Waiter	OK. So that's fresh English strawberries served with sugar and sweet champagne.

Interests and routines

1   Work in pairs. Find out about your partner's interests.

What	sort kind type	of	books films music	do you like?

I like ...	I don't like ...
I love ...	I hate ...

detective stories novels biographies history books science fiction others?	musicals thrillers comedies westerns horror films others?	jazz pop music classical music folk music rock music others?

2 1 Put the sports above with the right verb in the table below.

play	go	do

2 Think of some more sports. Which verbs do they go with?

3 What sports do other students take part in? Ask them.

Do you	play squash? go cycling? do aerobics?	Yes, I do No, I don't. Do you?		Where do you	play? go? do it?

3 Find out about a partner's routine.

Ask how often they

1 entertain customers or clients?   4 attend meetings?
2 use English at work?   5 travel abroad on business?
3 work overtime?   6 go jogging?

How often do you ... ?

Every	day two weeks month	Once a Twice a Three times a	week year

4

I always read the Financial Times.

I usually read the Economist.

I often read Time magazine, too.

I sometimes read the Wall Street Journal.

I don't often watch television.

I never watch cartoon films.

Find out about the person sitting next to you.
- What newspapers do they read?
- What magazines and journals do they read?
- What TV programmes do they watch?

Chatting

1 Work with a partner. Do this quiz and test your social English.

HOW GOOD IS YOUR SOCIAL ENGLISH?

Find out with this quiz. Decide which replies are possible.
(More than one reply may be OK.)

1 'Hello. How are you?'
  a I'm very fine, thank you.
  b Not too bad.
  c Fine thanks, and you?

2 'This is Stewart Edwards.'
  a How do you do?
  b How are you?
  c Pleased to meet you.

3 'Did you have a good trip?'
  a Yes, thanks.
  b Yes, of course.
  c Well, I had a few problems.

4 'Would you like to see round the factory?'
  a Yes, I will.
  b Yes, I'd love to.
  c No.

5 'Do you want to buy some?'
  a Well, I'm interesting.
  b Well, I'm interested.
  c Yes, I want.

6 'Why are you learning English?'
  a For talking to my customers.
  b For to talk to my customers.
  c To talk to my customers.

7 'Would you prefer red or white wine?'
  a I'd prefer red.
  b I don't care.
  c I don't mind.

8 'Is Thursday convenient?'
  a What means convenient?
  b What does convenient mean?
  c Could you explain me convenient?

9 'I'm terribly sorry about that.'
  a You're welcome.
  b Don't mention it.
  c Don't worry about it.

10 'Thank you very much.'
  a Not at all.
  b It doesn't matter.
  c It was a pleasure.

2 When you meet people for the first time, it's nice to find you've got things in common. Work with a partner. Do you both play golf? Do you both have the same number of children? Find five things you've got in common.

3   You go to a reception at an international conference in London. Talk to the other participants. Think of different replies.

4   Match these replies to the right comment.

a   Yes please. I'll have a gin and tonic.
b   Yes, it is. I didn't expect all this traffic.
c   It's very good of you but I'd like to walk.
d   Cheers.
e   That's right. I'm from Brazil.
f   Cheerio, then. See you tomorrow.
g   It's Emma. Emma Tanner.
h   Yes it is, isn't it?
i   Don't worry. I'll have an orange juice instead.
j   The Sheraton. It's not far from here.
k   Very good indeed, thank you.
l   Thanks. They look delicious.

SKILLS WORK

Speaking

You are having lunch with a foreign visitor to your company. You need to keep the conversation going.
- What subjects are easy to talk about?
- What subjects are interesting to talk about?
- What other subjects do you enjoy talking about?
  Add them to the list.

	easy	interesting
the work/business you are doing together		
your jobs		
your families		
your home towns		
sports		
your hobbies and interests		
the weather		
items in the news		
films		
your holidays		
politics		
religion		
love		

Find a colleague and compare your lists. Find a subject you both find interesting and have a conversation.

Reading

1 Before you read, imagine a typical British business executive.

What sports does he like?
What sort of home has he got?
What does he do in the evenings?
What's his favourite drink?
What sort of car does he drive?
Now read the article on the next page and see if you are right.

2 Answer these questions.
   1 What does a typical British executive do after dinner?
   2 What kinds of people did the researchers interview?
   3 What sorts of cars do European executives buy?

HIGHFLYING TASTES

The average British Executive has a game of squash or swim after work. Then he goes home to his detached house, washes up after dinner and sits down in front of the television with a scotch.

This is according to a survey on the different lifestyles of business people in thirteen different countries.

Researchers for the Pan European survey interviewed 8,604 professional people with a high income, education level or occupational status. Those interviewed were all aged between 25 and 74 and most of them were in the 35–44 age group.

The survey found that European executives have very different attitudes to life, but there is one thing on which they all agree. They are all patriotic when buying a car.

The British prefer Austin Rover and Ford, the French have Citroëns and Peugeots, the Germans have BMWs and Mercedes and the Italians have their Alfa Romeos and Fiats.

HOW THE EXECUTIVE LIFESTYLES COMPARE

%		Gt Britain	France	Germany	Italy	Netherlands	Spain	Sweden	Switzerland
TELEVISION	Watch under 7 hours	24.6	42.0	46.4	45.9	58.9	45.4	38.1	65.2
	7-14 hours	46.9	30.4	39.1	36.7	32.6	35.3	43.3	15.1
	15 hours or more	25.9	11.0	11.6	11.8	4.5	13.4	12.8	0.9
	Watch foreign stations	1.8	5.9	25.5	14.7	76.6	6.0	11.9	75.1
	Watch cable/satellite	2.2	3.3	18.7	1.7	44.0	4.5	10.9	22.8
LUXURIES	Own video recorder	65.5	40.0	44.2	29.9	40.7	48.2	42.0	34.5
	Video camera	7.2	8.7	9.7	9.7	4.6	19.4	10.7	11.6
	Compact disc player	16.7	25.4	28.2	26.2	23.7	44.2	17.2	34.6
	Car telephone	6.2	2.8	3.6	1.4	3.7	1.6	16.1	2.5
	Yacht/cruiser/speedboat	4.6	3.1	3.9	8.6	9.0	8.0	26.1	5.2
	Swimming pool	0.9	3.8	7.5	1.6	0.2	28.6	3.4	5.6
	Sauna	0.5	0.9	17.5	0.5	0.5	2.6	34.4	6.0
	Wear designer clothes	18.2	38.5	32.4	28.8	24.1	15.1	27.2	31.2
LEISURE	Foreign holidays	50.6	34.2	70.1	33.8	63.8	31.6	42.0	56.8
	Visits to the cinema	26.7	49.1	25.8	39.3	28.7	67.3	29.8	35.5
	Art galleries, museums	28.6	37.4	35.3	39.4	32.1	36.2	32.6	14.6
	Going to the theatre	35.4	24.5	40.3	30.5	33.3	32.0	32.1	33.8
	Swimming	65.5	42.8	56.2	44.1	42.6	49.9	36.6	50.7
	Cycling	24.1	29.4	52.2	12.9	33.6	11.6	13.3	30.8
	Tennis	23.1	31.9	33.8	28.4	33.4	33.4	21.1	26.1
DRINKING/SMOKING	Scotch	93.6	57.5	30.4	64.0	56.6	43.9	85.0	54.3
	Cognac	39.7	29.9	47.3	25.5	43.9	17.5	46.0	50.7
	Champagne	32.1	62.8	32.7	23.3	20.3	16.7	27.2	42.8
	Port	45.0	41.1	27.5	29.8	34.9	15.9	49.1	24.6
	Non-smokers	72.2	49.0	50.6	49.3	53.3	42.9	60.1	54.3

3 Ask a colleague questions about the statistics.

A *How many German executives go abroad on holiday?*
B *Seventy point one per cent.*

4 Is your country on the chart?

Yes? Do you think the statistics are accurate?
No? What do you think the statistics are in your country?

5 Write the questions the interviewers asked the executives.

How many hours do you spend watching television each week?
Do you watch any foreign stations?

Then use your questions to interview another student.

PRESENTATION

Three managers discuss the recruitment of sales representatives (reps) for their new Spanish sales organization.

1   ⟦19⟧ Listen and note their reaction to the alternatives. Write F if they are for them and A if they are against them.

Alternatives	Marcel	Carlos	Nancy
recruit new Spanish Sales reps			
transfer French Sales reps			

2   ⟦19⟧ Listen again and complete these minutes of the meeting.

Page 3

THE NEW SPANISH SALES ORGANIZATION

Alternative 1
Take on new Spanish sales representatives and .... [1].

Alternative 2
Teach our French sales reps Spanish and .... [2].

The advantage of Alternative 2 is the French sales staff have already got .... [3]. The disadvantage is it takes .... [4].

The disadvantage of Alternative 1 is that it takes a year to .... [5] On the other hand, it is a Spanish .... [6] so we should employ Spanish .... [7].

3 Match these phrases from the conversations to the correct box below.

a I don't agree.
b Why don't we … ?
c Any views on this?
d I think we should …
e I don't think we should …
f We need to discuss …
g What do you think?
h The important thing here is …
i How do you feel about that proposal … ?
j We can either … or …
k It's a waste of time.

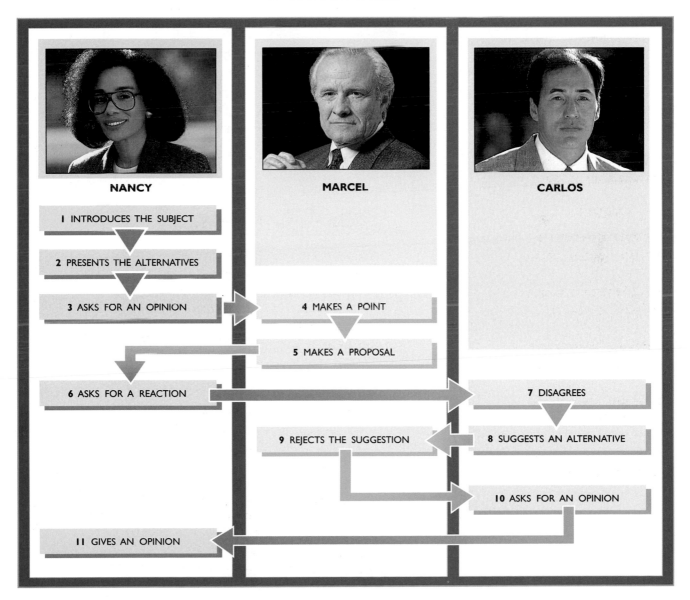

NANCY

MARCEL

CARLOS

1 INTRODUCES THE SUBJECT

2 PRESENTS THE ALTERNATIVES

3 ASKS FOR AN OPINION

4 MAKES A POINT

5 MAKES A PROPOSAL

6 ASKS FOR A REACTION

7 DISAGREES

9 REJECTS THE SUGGESTION

8 SUGGESTS AN ALTERNATIVE

10 ASKS FOR AN OPINION

11 GIVES AN OPINION

⃞19 Now listen to the conversations again and check your answers.

LANGUAGE WORK

Recommending action

1 Recommend action in these situations. Begin your sentences with:
I think we should … or I don't think we should …

1 You have a machine that is old and often breaks down.
2 Your market share is falling.
3 One of your suppliers often sends you invoices with several mistakes on them.
4 The company's main warehouse is too small.
5 Your main competitors are cutting their prices by 20%.
6 An employee is often absent from work. He says he's ill but you don't believe him.

2 Work with a colleague. You are meeting to discuss some of your company's problems. Take it in turns to start discussions on these subjects.

A *We need to discuss …*
  Basically, we've got two alternatives. We can either … or …
  What do you think?
B *I think we should …*

PROBLEM	ALTERNATIVES	
company English classes	employ a teacher	send the staff to a language school
the paperwork	buy another computer	recruit a secretary
company cars	rent them	buy them
the pay deal	offer a 10% salary increase	offer 5% and a productivity bonus
office cleaning	employ cleaners	outsource the work
the new sales job	promote someone	contact a recruitment agency

Asking for opinions

1 People often disagree about politics. Do you agree (A) or disagree (D) with these views?

Speaker's Corner, Hyde Park, London

☐ 1 The government should spend less money on defence.

☐ 2 We should have compulsory military service.

☐ 3 There should be higher taxes on petrol.

☐ 4 The government should invest in renewable forms of energy.

☐ 5 There should be lower taxes on cigarettes.

☐ 6 The government should spend more on education.

☐ 7 We should have more police patrolling the streets.

☐ 8 There should be tighter immigration controls.

2 Compare your opinions about the views above with a partner.

Do you think ... ?	Yes, I do because ... No, I don't because ...
I think ...	I agree because ... I disagree because ...

3 Now tell some partners your views on privatization. Use the chart to make sentences and then ask for their views.

What do you think?
How do you feel about this?
Have you got any views on this?

I think I don't think	we should	privatize nationalize	telecommunications. the railways. industries like water and electricity. the army. the police force.
	we should have there should be	private	schools. hospitals. prisons.

Making suggestions | Study these ways of making suggestions.

MAKING SUGGESTIONS	ACCEPTING	REJECTING
Why don't we ... ? *Shall we ... ?* *We could ...*	*That's a good idea.* *Yes, let's do that.* *Great.*	*Yes, but ...* *That's a good idea but ...* *I'm not sure about that.*

Practise the phrases with a colleague. Suggest solutions to the problems below. Follow this pattern:

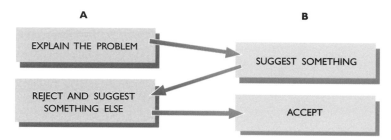

1   You need to improve your staff's English. What can you do?
2   Your company's results show an unexpected $500,000 profit on international currency deals. Suggest things to do with the money.
3   You need to think of a name for your new brand of toothpaste. Suggest some alternatives.
4   You work for a bank. You want to attract more young customers aged between 5 and 18. How can you do it?
5   Your company was founded 100 years ago. You want to mark the occasion. Suggest ways to celebrate.

Justifying decisions | We use *going to* to talk about things we plan to do in the future.

It takes five hours to drive to Budapest so I'm going to fly.

Complete these sentences in a similar way. Use *going to* or *not going to* and the words in brackets.
1   They've got one meeting in Madrid on Tuesday afternoon and another on Wednesday morning so they ...
    (hotel overnight)
2   His flight left late, so he ...
    (on time)
3   I've got my car with me so I ...
    (a drink)
4   She can't attend the meeting so she ...
    (her assistant instead)
5   Sales are down so you ...
    (good results this year)
6   The last time we parked there we got a ticket so we ...
    (somewhere else)

For more information on future forms see page 170.

2   Your company wants to improve the quality of its product/service. Your boss wants you to organize regular meetings to discuss ways to achieve this objective. Decide how the meetings should be run. Choose a or b, or invent your own answer.

1   Are you going to
a   invite staff from all levels of the organization?
b   just invite managers?
c   ....
....

2   Are you going to
a   decide who should attend?
b   ask for volunteers
c   ....
....

3   Are you going to
a   hold the meetings once a week?
b   hold the meetings once a month?
c   ....
....

4   Are you going to
a   hold the meetings in office hours?
b   hold the meetings in the evenings or at weekends?
c   ....
....

5   Are you going to
a   keep the meetings short?
b   allow the meetings to go on as long as necessary?
c   ....
....

6   Are you going to
a   allow people to smoke?
b   stop people smoking?
c   ....
....

Justify your decisions to a colleague.
A   *Why are you going to... ?*
B   *I'm going to... because...*
      I'm not going to... because...

Pronunciation

1 [20] Listen to the first halves of some of the sentences below. Choose the correct ending, then listen to the complete sentences and check your answers.

1 We're going to walk ... to the meeting.
   We're going to work ... together in a joint venture.
2 We're going to sit ... down and start the meeting now.
   We're going to seat ... ten people round the table.
3 We're going to halve ... the budget.
   We're going to have ... a long discussion.
4 We're going to look ... at some figures.
   We're going to lock ... the door.
5 We're going to leave ... at five o'clock.
   We're going to live ... in Oxford.

2 Practise the sentences with a partner. One person should read a first half. The other should listen carefully and say the correct ending.

Problem solving

1 Simo Hattari needs English for his work, but he has a problem.

'Everyone at work has the same problem as me. We don't get enough opportunities to practise speaking English. I can watch quite a lot of English programmes on Finnish TV so my listening is quite good but I'd really like to speak more.'

Do you have a similar problem? What do you think Simo should do?

A *I think he should talk to his colleagues about this problem. They should arrange to speak English to each other sometimes.*
B *They should try holding meetings in the company in English.*
C *I don't think they should do that. It's too difficult. I think he should try to meet some English and American people.*

2 Read some more people's problems. (Do you have similar problems yourself?) What do you think they should do?

1 'When foreign visitors come to our office, I can't understand them. I ask them to speak slowly, but it's still difficult. My English teacher says my pronunciation is difficult to understand too, but I think my main problem is listening. I need more practice.'

2 'I have a very busy working day and often I'm still in the office at eight or nine at night. But English is our company language so I have to learn it. I study for half an hour every night when I get home. The trouble is I'm not making fast enough progress.'

3 'My teacher says people can learn a language at any age but I'm not sure that's true. My memory is the problem. I'm getting old and I find it difficult to remember new English words.'

4 'I'm nervous about speaking English on the telephone. It's difficult when you can't see the person you're talking to. There are lots of long pauses while I think what to say.'

5 'I have to attend meetings that are held in English with our suppliers. I know what I want to say but I can't find the right words. I often have to use ten words instead of one. My vocabulary is too small. I need to learn more words.'

3   Now read how the people plan to solve their problems. Match these solutions to the correct problem. Are they going to do any of the things you suggested? Do you think they are good solutions?

a   'Before I make a call, I'm going to make a note of what I want to say. I can look up any words I don't know in a dictionary. I'll feel more confident.'

b   'I'm going to get up half an hour earlier in the mornings and study English then. I think better first thing. It's "quality" time.'

c   'I'm going to subscribe to cable TV. It's not going to be easy to follow the programs at first, but the pictures will help me understand what's happening. My teacher thinks it's going to improve my pronunciation, too.'

d   'I'm going to start reading more. There's an English newspaper I can buy that has some words translated. I'm going to start with that and I'll write down new words that look useful and test myself on them.'

e   'I've got a book called *How to Improve Your Memory* and there are several good techniques in it. They're things like using rhymes and dreaming up funny mental pictures. I think I can use them in my English lessons. I'm also going to review what we learn more often.'

SKILLS WORK

Listening and writing

1 ⏺21a Listen to part of a meeting and complete these notes.

Proposal: *Special catalogue for multimedia products*
Action plan:
Person responsible:
Review date:

2 ⏺21b Now listen to another part of the meeting and complete these notes.

Proposal:
Action plan:
Person responsible:
Review date:

3 ⏺21 Listen again if necessary, and supply alternative words in these sentences. Use words from the meeting.

1 We need to | calculate
w.......... o.......... | the costs.

2 Could you | handle
d.......... w.......... | that, Thierry?

3 Could you | tell us about it?
f.......... u.......... i.......... ? |

4 Customers can't | be connected
g.......... t.......... | after six o'clock.

5 Do you want to | recruit
t.......... o.......... | more sales staff?

6 Ulrike, can you | organize
t.......... c.......... o.......... | it?

Speaking **1** Your company must reduce its running costs by £1,000,000. How are you going to save the money? Look at the proposals and decide.

```
           ESTIMATED SAVINGS


1 Cut the research and development budget:
                                        ------------
                      by 5%     £400,000
                      by 10%    £800,000
                                        ------------

2 Cut the staff training budget:
                                        ------------
                      by 10%    £200,000
                      by 20%    £400,000
                                        ------------

3 Cut the advertising budget:
                                        ------------
                      by 10%    £350,000
                      by 20%    £700,000
                                        ------------
                                        ------------
4 Stop all donations to charity:  £100,000
                                        ------------

5 Make the company security
  staff redundant and                   ------------
  outsource the work:              £150,000
                                        ------------
                                        ------------
6 Close the company health centre: £100,000
                                        ------------

7 Cancel the plans to buy:
                                        ------------
  new production machinery         £200,000
  new computer equipment           £150,000
                                        ------------
```

2 Hold a meeting with some colleagues. Discuss the proposals one by one and decide what to do.

If you decide to make a cut, decide who is responsible for taking action, and when by.

Who is going to be responsible for this?
Can you deal with that?
Could you take care of this?
How soon can you do it?
Good. Can we discuss this again next Monday, then?

OBJECTIVE

to make and change
arrangements

TASKS

to explain future plans
and arrangements

•

to fix a time and place
for a meeting

•

to invite business
contacts to social
events

•

to write a fax message
arranging a visit

•

to arrange a schedule
for a visit

PRESENTATION

I [22] Listen to three telephone calls Alan Wilson received and fill in
the details in his diary below.

2 Listen to the three calls again and answer these questions.
[22a]

1 Patrick invites Alan to play golf. What does he say?
....

2 At the end of the call he confirms the arrangement. What does he
say?
....

[22b]

3 Mrs Lonsdale invites Alan to her office to see some plans. What
does she say?
....

4 Why can't Alan go on Friday?
....

5 At the end of the call she confirms the arrangement. What does
she say?
....

22c

6 Cristina tells Alan she can't keep her appointment on the 16th. What does she say?

....

7 Why can't Alan meet her on the 18th? What does he say?

....

3 After the last phone call, Alan picked up the phone and made another call. Who did he ring and what did he say?

Pronunciation

1 23a Intonation is very important in English. If your voice is flat, you can sound bored or rude. Listen to some phrases from the conversations spoken twice. Is the intonation good or is it flat?

	good	flat
1 Hello, nice to hear from you.	☐	☐
Hello, nice to hear from you.	☐	☐
2 That's a good idea.	☐	☐
That's a good idea.	☐	☐
3 Yes, that's fine.	☐	☐
Yes, that's fine.	☐	☐
4 That would be nice.	☐	☐
That would be nice.	☐	☐
5 Fine. Thank you for calling.	☐	☐
Fine. Thank you for calling.	☐	☐

2 23b Listen to the phrases in a conversation, then practise reading it with a partner. Make sure your intonation isn't flat.

Hello, Pat. It's Chris here. ...
Pat, do you feel like a game of golf? ...
How about Thursday morning then? 10 o'clock? ...
And would you like to have lunch afterwards? ...
Good. See you on Thursday, then. ...

Dates

1 24 How do we say this date in English: 6/10/98?

Listen to a British and American person discussing it. What's the problem?
Notice that British people say *the* and *of* when they are giving dates, but they do not use *the* and *of* when they write them.

2 Write down some special dates, for example birthdays, anniversaries, historical dates. Dictate them to a colleague. They should write them down and guess why they are special.

LANGUAGE WORK

Timetables, plans, and arrangements

1 We often use the Present Simple tense to talk about timetables. Work with a partner, asking and answering questions.

A *When does the London train leave?*
B *It leaves at 11.20.*

The London train	leave arrive	11.20 a.m. 3.45 p.m.
The meeting	start finish	3.00 p.m. 5.15 p.m.
The bank	open close	9.30 a.m. 3.30 p.m.

2 Now look at the conference programme and ask about

- the Regional Performance Reports
- shuttle buses to the airport
- Mange Tout Restaurant
- the Roof-Top Barbecue
- Highlights hairdressers
- coach tours of the city.

IAMT CONFERENCE

PROGRAMME FOR JULY 22ND

9.30 am	Regional Performance Reports: Germany Italy Scandinavia Marlborough Room Conference Suite 6th Floor
12.30 p.m.	Lunch Swithins Restaurant 3rd Floor
2.30 p.m.	Regional Performance Reports: The USA Hungary Spain Marlborough Room Conference Suite 6th Floor
8.00 p.m. - Midnight	Roof-Top Barbecue with the 'Hill Runners Jazz Quartet' Riverside Hotel Roof Garden

SHUTTLEBUSES TO THE AIRPORT (SHUTTLEBUS)

Riverside Hotel offers a regular daily service to Heathrow and Gatwick. Coaches leave from the main entrance at 7.00, 10.00, 13.00, 16.00 and 19.00.

Please allow 60 minutes for your journey to Heathrow and 90 minutes for Gatwick.

MANGE TOUT RESTAURANT
FRENCH CUISINE

Lunch
12 noon – 2.30 p.m.

Dinner
7.00 p.m. – 11.00 p.m.

The restaurant is located in the Florence Arcade on the Ground Floor. Patrons are kindly requested to reserve a table in advance to avoid disappointment.
(01751) 248260

HIGHLIGHTS
UNISEX HAIRDRESSERS

9.45 a.m.–5.30 p.m.
Florence Arcade
Riverside Hotel
01751-248197

No appointment necessary

★ ★ ★ ★ ★ ★ ★ ★ ★ ★ ★ ★
COACH TOURS OF THE CITY

Twice daily tours
10.30–12.30; 2.30–4.30

£8 adult £5 child
Please book at reception

3   Look at the itinerary below. Ask and answer questions about Mr Gruber's schedule.

A *When is he arriving?*
B *At nine o'clock.*
A *What's he doing first?*
B *He's meeting the Overseas Sales Manager in the conference room.*

```
         ITINERARY FOR THE VISIT OF MR H. GRUBER TO THE
                       LEYTONSTONE FACTORY
                            25 JULY

9.00            Arrival
9.05-9.45       Meeting with the Overseas Sales Manager
                (Conference Room)
9.45-10.15      Coffee with the Marketing Director and
                Finance Director
10.15-10.45     Company presentation video
10.45-11.45     Demonstration of the N4 prototype
11.45-12.40     Meeting with the Managing Director and
                Marketing Director     (Boardroom)
12.40-2.30      Lunch with the Overseas Sales Manager
                (Saraceno Restaurant)
2.30-3.30       Tour of Leytonstone factory
3.30-4.00       Final discussions with the Overseas
                Sales Manager
4.00            Car to Terminal 2, Heathrow Airport
6.00            Flight to Frankfurt, LH 1607
```

We often use the Present Continuous tense to talk about future plans and arrangements. For more information, see page 167.

Making appointments

1   Put these sentences in the correct order to make a short conversation.

☐ Yes, please. Would Tuesday the 26th be convenient?
☐ Good morning, Mrs Mane. This is Peter Brien.
☐ It's quite all right. I'll look forward to seeing you on Thursday the 28th, then.
☐ I'm calling about our appointment on the 25th. I'm afraid I can't make it.
☐ Fine. Thank you. Goodbye.
☐ Good morning, Mr Brien. How can I help you?
☐ Yes, I can manage the 28th. I'm sorry to be a nuisance.
☑ Shifali Mane.
☐ It's not a problem. Would you like to fix another time, then?
☐ I'm afraid I'm tied up on the 26th. How about the 28th?

25   Listen and check your answers.

2 Supply alternative words for these phrases. Use words from the conversation.

1 We need to | arrange f.......... | a time for the meeting.

2 | Are you free H.......... .... | next Wednesday?

3 I'm afraid I'm | busy. t.......... up. |

4 When would | suit you? be c.......... ? |

5 I can | make m.......... | Friday.

6 I'm afraid I can't | come m.......... it | to Tuesday's meeting.

3 Complete these sentences with words from the box.

| make   cancel   be late for   have   postpone |

1 My name is George Rawlings and I _____ an appointment to see Mrs Bernejo at 2.30.
2 She's always very punctual so I don't want to _____ our appointment.
3 I'd like to _____ an appointment to see the manager.
4 Mr Cottage is ill so we need to _____ his appointments.
5 I'm sorry to be a nuisance but could we _____ our appointment until next week?

4 Sometimes we have to *cancel* or *postpone* appointments. What other things do we cancel or postpone? Make up more sentences using the verbs *cancel* and *postpone* then turn to File 10 on page 159.

Invitations

1 You are entertaining a foreign visitor from your parent company. Ask if they want to

- come to the monthly marketing meeting
- give a talk at the meeting
- meet the production manager
- see the new packaging machinery
- come to a party.

Use the phrases in the table opposite.

INVITING	SAYING *YES*	SAYING *NO*
Would you like to … ?	Thank you. I'd like that. That would be lovely.	I'd love to but… I'm sorry, but …

2 Compare these phrases with the ones above. Which are more informal?

INVITING	SAYING *YES*	SAYING *NO*
Do you feel like … -ing? How about … -ing?	That's a good idea. Yeah, great.	Well, actually … I'm afraid …

3 Ask a colleague about their future plans. If they are free, invite them to do something with you.

A *Are you doing anything special tonight?*
B *No, not really. I'm just going home and watching TV.*
A *How about coming out for a drink?*
B *That's a good idea.*

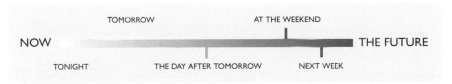

Here are some ideas of things to do. Can you think of any more?

Fixing a time

I Study these phrases for fixing a time.

SUGGESTING A TIME		
Can you	make manage	2 o'clock on Thursday?
How about		
Are you free	on the 26th? at 3.30?	

SAYING YES	SAYING NO			
Yes, that suits me. Yes, I'm free. Yes, that's fine.	I'm afraid	I can't	make manage	it.
	I'm tied up.			

Practise the phrases in pairs. Use the pattern below.

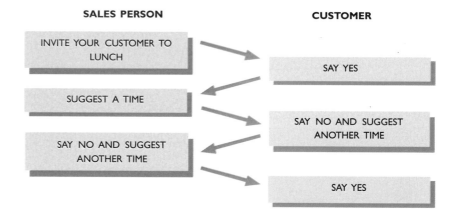

Now practise again. The sales person should invite the customer to
- visit a local tourist spot
- come to dinner
- come to a night-club.

2 You want to arrange a meeting with the people sitting next to you. Arrange a time and place that suits everyone.

ASKING FOR SUGGESTIONS		
When	would	suit you?
What time		
Where		be convenient for you?

CONFIRMING
I'll look forward to seeing you on Thursday at ten, then.
See you on Thursday at ten, then.

3 Work in pairs. One person should look at the information below and the other should look at the information in File 19 on page 161.

You want to arrange a meeting with your colleague. Phone him/her and arrange a time and place. Here is your diary for next week.

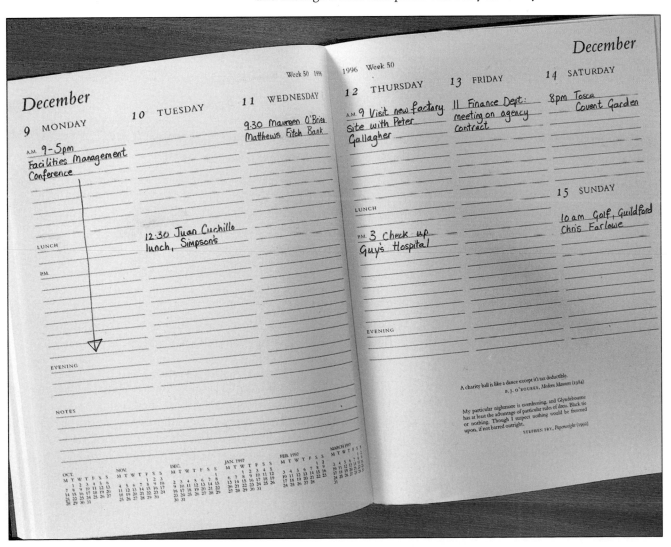

SKILLS WORK

Writing

1 Read this fax. What is it about?

NIHON INFORMALINK KK

INFORMALINK BLDG, 2-4-8 KANAMECHO, TOSHIMA-KU, TOKYO 171

TELEPHONE: (6) 5995 3801/4 TELEFAX: (6) 5995 3919

```
To:   Darworth Enterprises    Attention:  Janet Jeffries
From: Masahiro Nakagawa       Re:  My inspection visit
Date: 10 June                 Pages including this one:  1
```

```
Thank you for you fax of 1 June.
I will be arriving on Flight no. JL 401 at Terminal 3
Heathrow on 16th June. Could you book hotel accommodation
for three nights in the city centre? Also, I would be
grateful if you could arrange a meeting with Data Link for
me on June 17th if possible.
I look forward to seeing you on the 16th.
Kind regards,
```

Masahiro Nakagawa

```
Masahiro Nakagawa
```

Compare the style and layout of this fax with the letters on page 27. How is it similar and how is it different?

2 Faxes and letters are very similar. But information about the receiver appears at the top of the fax message so there is often no greeting. Also people often say *Regards* or *Kind regards* at the end.

Practise writing some faxes. Work in two groups. One group should use the information below. The other group should use the information in File 11 on page 159.

1   You are Janet Jeffries. Write a fax in reply to Mr Nakagawa's fax. (One person in the group should write and the others should dictate and check spellings.)

Thank him for his fax. Tell him you will meet him at Heathrow at 16.35 on June 16. As requested, you booked a single room for him in the Dorchester Hotel for two nights. Check this is OK. (If his wife is coming too, you need to change the booking.)
You also arranged his meeting with Data Link for June 17th. Say you'll see him next week, send your regards and sign the message from 'Janet Jeffries'.

2   You will receive a message from the other group. Write a reply.

Speaking

Work with a partner. One person should use the information below and the other should use the information in File 29 on page 164.

1 You are visiting your UK subsidiary for three days next week. You have two lunch-time appointments but you also want to arrange meetings with the people on this list.

NAMES	TIME NEEDED FOR MEETING
Mrs Carne	3 hours (must see her on Monday morning)
Mr Gandhi	2 hours
Miss Carley	3 hours
Mr Barnes	4 hours (factory tour)
Ms Lyon	2 hours (Wednesday if possible)

Phone your colleague in the UK and arrange your schedule. Pencil in the times.

MONDAY 21	TUESDAY 22	WEDNESDAY 23
9–10am	9–10am	9–10am
10–11am	10–11am	10–11am
11–12am	11–12am	11–12am
12–1pm *lunch with Dave Czernovicz (Barclays Bank)*	12–1pm *Reception Barbican Centre*	12–1pm
1–2pm	1–2pm	1–2pm
2–3pm	2–3pm	2–3pm
3–4pm	3–4pm	3–4pm
4–5pm	4–5pm	4–5pm

2 Your boss has just told you about an important meeting at head office. You must change your plans so you can catch the 6 a.m. flight home on Wednesday morning. Phone your colleague in the UK again. Explain your problem and rearrange your schedule.

You can cancel your visit to the reception at the Barbican Centre, but you can't cancel your appointment with Dave Czernovicz.

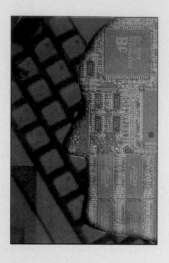

OBJECTIVE

to describe and discuss
figures and graphs

TASKS

to describe changes in
a company's finances

•

to analyse figures and
give reasons for rises
and falls

•

to describe and explain
trends in your
workplace

•

to read about the
growth of a
multinational

PRESENTATION

1 Complete these graphs.

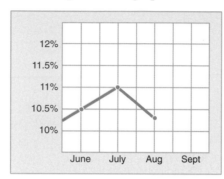

1 The rate of unemployment increased
to 11% in September.

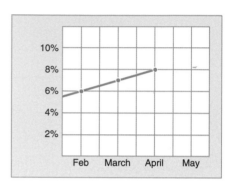

2 Interest rates decreased by 2% in May.

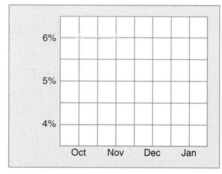

3 Inflation went down from 5.5% in
December to 5% in January.

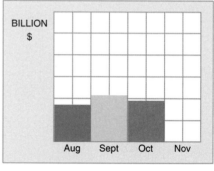

4 Consumer spending rose sharply in
November.

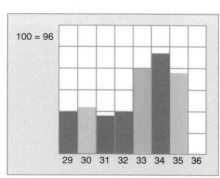

5 The retail price index went up slightly
in week 36.

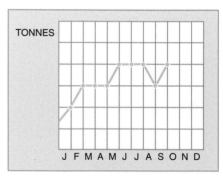

6 Production fell steadily in the last
quarter of the year.

2 [26] Listen to a sales manager describing his company's sales figures
and complete the graph opposite.

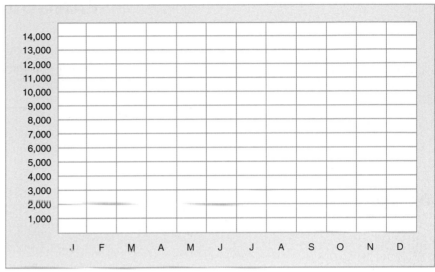

3 26 Listen again and note why these things happened.

1 Sales increased in March.

....

2 Sales fell in May.

....

3 Sales rose in July.

....

4 Sales increased in September.

....

5 Sales went down in November.

....

4 Complete these sentences about the sales figures. Use a preposition (*to, from, by, at, etc.*)

1 Sales stayed _____ 6000 in February.
2 They increased _____ 7000 in March _____ 8000 in April.
3 They decreased _____ 3000 in May.
4 They fell _____ 4000 in June.
5 They rose _____ 5000 _____ 6000 in August.
6 They increased _____ 7000 between August and October.
7 They remained steady _____ 7000 in December.

5 Complete these sentences with the correct preposition.

1	We	invested	a lot of money	_____ the business.
2		spent		_____ training courses.
3		wasted		_____ unnecessary equipment.
4		made		_____ our overseas investments.
5		saved		_____ our energy bills.
6		gave		_____ charity.
7		borrowed		_____ the bank.
8		owed		_____ our suppliers.

LANGUAGE WORK

Rises and falls

1 Discuss these figures with a colleague. One person should use the information on the left and the other should use the information on the right. Use these verbs.

increase
rise
go up

decrease
fall
go down

A Our market share fell by 1% last year.
B Yes, but on the other hand our turnover increased by 8%.

Our market share	-1%	Our turnover	+8%
Distribution costs	+18%	Prices of raw materials	-4%
The number of new contracts	-6%	Spending on research and development	+9%
Earnings from investments	-3%	Debts to our suppliers	-4%
The number of employees	-4%	Productivity	+6%
Sales to the EC	-2%	Sales to South America	+5%
Wages	+8%	Our staff turnover	-20%
Spending on training	+15%	Customer complaints	-16%

2 Write six sentences describing rises and falls in your company's figures. (You can invent statistics you don't know.)

Our turnover increased by 50 million francs last year.
The number of employees went up by five per cent.

Pronunciation

1 The spelling of English words is often different from their pronunciation. We sometimes write letters we don't pronounce. For example, *debt* is pronounced /det/. The 'b' is silent.

How do we pronounce these English words? Cross out the silent letters like this: *debt*

1	write	5	listen	9	half
2	know	6	high	10	scientist
3	answer	7	sign	11	chemist
4	receipt	8	business	12	psychiatrist

2 27 Listen and check your answers.

Describing changes

1 Complete these tables.

VERB *(action)*	NOUN *(thing)*
to rise	a rise
to fall	_____
to increase	_____
to decrease	_____
to improve	_____
to recover	_____

Now complete this table.

ADJECTIVE *(describes a noun)*	ADVERB *(describes a verb)*
slight	slightly
sharp	_____
dramatic	_____
steady	_____

Which adjective describes:
1 a sudden, very large change?
2 a sudden, large change?
3 a very small change?
4 a regular change (not sudden)?

2 Study the graph and use each adjective once to complete the description.

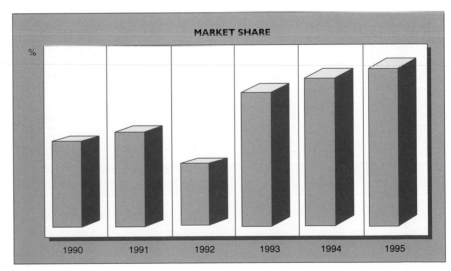

We had a _____ ¹ increase in market share in 1991, followed by a _____ ² fall in 1992, when we sold a brand. But a successful new brand launched in 1993 meant there was a _____ ³ recovery that year, and a _____ ⁴ increase in 1994 and 1995 too.

3   Now use each adverb once to complete this description.

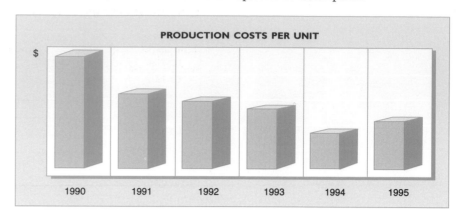

Our production costs per unit fell _____¹ in 1991 when we automated the assembly line and they continued to decrease _____² for the next three years.

They went down _____³ in 1994 when we bought the new packaging machinery but rose _____⁴ in 1995 because of increased time spent on quality control.

4   Now use each adverb and adjective once to complete this description.

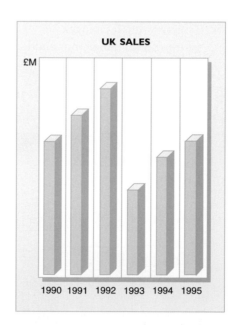
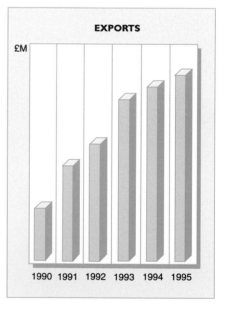

Sales to the UK market rose _____¹ between 1990 and 1992. There was a _____² decrease in 1993 when our main distributor went out of business. Sales rose _____³ in 1994, and the _____⁴ improvement in 1995 brought us back to the 1990 level.

There was a _____⁵ rise in exports in 1991. They went up _____⁶ in 1992 when we began to break into the US market.

They rose _____⁷ in 1993 when we signed the new agency agreements and there was a _____⁸ increase in 1994 and 1995.

Describing graphs

Work in pairs. One person should use the information below and the other should use the information in File 23 on page 162.

The graph below shows a company's sales over a twelve-month period. Describe it to your partner. They should draw it.

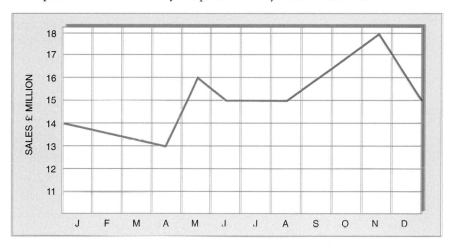

Now listen to your partner's description of the energy costs of a smaller company over a period of twelve months. Draw the graph.

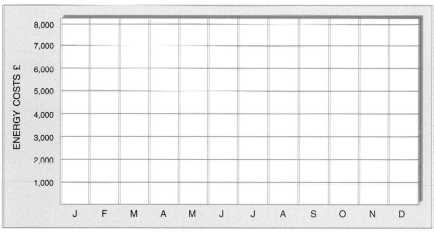

Giving reasons

1 Look at the figures below. In which month did these events happen?

	month
1 the autumn mail shot	*September*
2 a spell of cold weather	
3 a move to larger premises	
4 the installation of a call routing system	
5 the launch party for the new season's designs	
6 the annual sales conference in Brussels	

Bradford Branch

Overheads	July £	Aug £	Sept £	Oct £	Nov £	Dec £
Rent	690	950	950	950	950	950
Gas and Electricity charges	560	560	600	1300	700	900
Postage costs	600	610	1500	590	630	580
Travel costs	250	400	320	12800	590	280
Telephone charges	460	490	280	280	290	270
Entertainment costs	640	520	500	490	2100	650

2 Work with a partner. Ask and answer questions about the figures.

A *Why was there a rise in rent in August?*
B *That was because of a move to larger premises.*

3 Write some sentences explaining the figures.

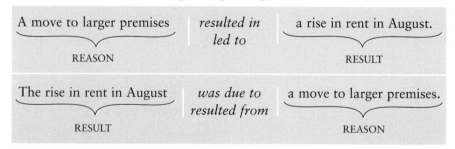

A move to larger premises	*resulted in* *led to*	a rise in rent in August.
REASON		RESULT
The rise in rent in August	*was due to* *resulted from*	a move to larger premises.
RESULT		REASON

4 Study the sentences below. Which are reasons and which are results? Link them with one of the phrases above.

1 The factory automation .... an increase in productivity.
2 The staff reductions .... the factory automation.
3 The large pay rises .... a decrease in staff turnover.
4 The increase in sales costs .... the rise in spending on advertising.
5 The big orders from Japan .... a recovery in sales.
6 The shorter delivery times .... the new distribution system.
7 The increase in competition .... a decrease in our market share.
8 The rise in distribution costs .... the increase in petrol prices.

SKILLS WORK

Speaking **I** Draw a graph representing something connected with your work, for example

- seasonal sales trends
- annual turnover
- raw materials prices
- number of employees.

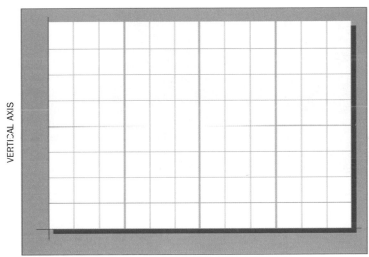

VERTICAL AXIS

HORIZONTAL AXIS

2 Work in pairs or small groups. Take it in turns to present your graphs to one another.

- Explain what they represent.
- Give reasons for the changes.
- Answer questions.

These phrases will help you.

This graph shows …	*As you can see …*
This led to …	*This resulted in …*
This was due to …	*This resulted from …*
Are there any questions?	

Reading **I** What do you know about The Coca-Cola Company?
Do you know the story of:

- the inventor of Coke?
- the famous Coca-Cola contour bottle?
- the secret formula?
- Coke and World War II?
- 'New Coke'?

*'Coca-Cola' and 'Coke' are registered trade marks of
The Coca-Cola Company*

THE STORY OF COKE

Dr Styth Pemberton, the pharmacist who produced Coca-Cola in his backyard.

1   Dr John Styth Pemberton made it in his backyard, took it to his local pharmacy, and they put it on sale at 5 cents a glass. Hand-painted signs saying 'Coca-Cola' appeared outside the store and inside
5   signs invited customers to 'Drink'. But sales didn't take off. In the first year they averaged just 9 drinks a day.

He thought it would never be very successful and he steadily sold his shares in the business to different
10   partners. In 1888, just before he died, he sold his last shares to Asa G. Candler, a businessman from Atlanta.

He distributed thousands of coupons for a complimentary glass of Coca-Cola and he promoted
15   the drink with souvenir fans, calendars, clocks, and novelties. Sales rose dramatically and, by 1892, they were ten times their 1888 level.

Coca-Cola had to develop a bottling system and set up plants. The first bottling plant opened in Vicksburg in 1894 and over the next 25 years, the   20 number of plants rose from two to over a thousand. Other soft drink companies tried to imitate the Coca-Cola taste so the company kept the drink's formula secret and searched for a distinctive package. In 1916, they introduced the first bottle   25 with the famous Coca-Cola shape.

Then the United States joined the war, and the company President gave an order 'to see that every man in uniform gets a bottle of Coca-Cola for 5 cents, wherever he is and whatever the cost to the   30 company.' As a result, Coca-Cola shipped 64 bottling plants abroad during the war. And when the war finished, they were ready to conquer the world. From the mid 1940s until 1960, the number of countries with bottling plants nearly doubled.   35

This was the first change in the secret formula since 1886. In pre-launch tests, consumers preferred the new taste. But the tests couldn't measure their feelings for the brand. Coca-Cola had a special place in their hearts and they didn't want a change. For the   40 first time in history, sales of Coca-Cola fell. The company responded quickly and marketed the original formula again as Coca-Cola Classic. Sales climbed back up again, and continued to grow.

And if you're not sure what the world's top selling   45 soft drink is by now; 'Coke is it'.

Jacob's Pharmacy in Atlanta where Coca-Cola was first sold.

Most early bottling plants had a small staff and only operated in summer when demand was high.

Robert Woodruff, the Coca-Cola Company president laid the foundations for the international success of Coca-Cola during the war. He ordered that every man in uniform should be able to get a glass of Coca-Cola for 5 cents, no matter where he was or what the cost was.

These photographs are reproduced with kind permission from The Coca-Cola Company.

2 The first sentence in each paragraph of this article is missing. They are all listed below. Read the article and decide where each sentence goes.

1 Asa Candler had a talent for marketing.
2 In the 1980s, in the USA only, the company launched a new taste for Coke.
3 In 1941, there were bottling plants in 44 countries.
4 Coca-Cola was invented in Atlanta, Georgia on May 8, 1886.
5 So today millions of people all over the world are drinking Coke.
6 The huge increase in the popularity of the drink led to problems meeting demand.
7 Dr Pemberton didn't see the potential of his new drink.

Notice how the sentences introduce the topic of the paragraphs.

3 If you don't understand a new word, try looking carefully at the words around it. You can often work out what sort of word it is and what it means.

… a complimentary glass of Coca-Cola …
Complimentary is an adjective – it means *free*.

… to imitate the Coca-Cola taste…
Imitate is a verb – it means *copy*.

Look at the story again and try to guess what these words mean.

a signs   (line 3)
b take off   (line 6)
c shares   (line 9)
d coupons   (line 13)
e bottling plants   (line 19)
f shape   (line 26)
g abroad   (line 32)
h conquer   (line 33)
i brand   (line 39)
j responded   (line 42)

4 Work with a colleague. Ask and answer questions about the story of Coca-Cola. Use these words.

Who … ?
When … ?
Why … ?
Where … ?
What … ?
How … ?

OBJECTIVE

to discuss recent work activities and report on progress

TASKS

to give news about a company's recent financial results

•

to report on progress in achieving targets

•

to explain recent changes in staffing levels

•

to follow the radio business news

•

to review an investment portfolio

PRESENTATION

1   Who services the equipment and machinery in your company? And who fixes it when it breaks down?

2 Study these performance figures for an office equipment repair company.

1 How many call-outs did they receive in September?
2 How soon do they try to answer their customers' calls?
3 How soon do they try to repair their machines?
4 Did they achieve their targets in September?

	SEPTEMBER		
	CALL-OUTS	CALLS ANSWERED WITHIN 4 HOURS	MACHINES REPAIRED WITHIN 24 HOURS
NUMBER	803	679	738
PERCENTAGE		84.6%	91.9%
TARGET		80%	90%
DIFFERENCE		+4.6%	+1.9%

	OCTOBER		
	CALL-OUTS	CALLS ANSWERED WITHIN 4 HOURS	MACHINES REPAIRED WITHIN 24 HOURS
NUMBER			
PERCENTAGE		80%	83.2%
TARGET		80%	90%
DIFFERENCE		0%	-6.8%

3 ⊞28 You will hear two people discussing October's figures. Listen and complete the table.

4 Why haven't they achieved their repair target this month?

5 ⊞28 Read the first part of the conversation and try to remember the words that are missing. Fill them in using one word per space. Then listen again and check your answers.

A _____ _____ have you got with our performance figures. Have you finished them _____?
B Yes, _____ _____.
A Good. How do they compare with last month's?
B The number of call-outs _____ _____up.
A I thought so. _____ _____ very busy.
B It's _____ to 880. Last month it was 803 so it's 77 up.
A Have we _____ the targets? That's the question.

LANGUAGE WORK

Giving news | **1** Graphic Images has just published its annual profit and loss account. Match these explanations to the correct items.

1 money paid to the shareholders
2 the cost of delivering goods to the customers
3 the money kept in the company and added to the reserves
4 the cost of managing the company
5 the cost of raw materials and manufacturing

GRAPHIC IMAGES PLC

CONSOLIDATED PROFIT AND LOSS ACCOUNT

	THIS YEAR £m	LAST YEAR £m
Home Sales	189	175
Export Sales	181	191
Total Sales	370	366
Cost of Sales	(254)	(255)
Gross Profit	116	111
Distribution Costs	(17)	(17)
Administrative Costs	(35)	(30)
Profit before tax	64	64
Tax	(23)	(22)
Profit after tax	41	42
Dividend	(36)	(34)
Retained profit	5	8

2 Work with a colleague. Ask and answer questions about the figures.

A *What's happened to sales this year?*
B *They've* | *increased.*
　　　　　　　| *gone up.*
　　　　　　　| *risen.*

A *What about profit after tax?*
B *It's* | *decreased.*
　　　　　| *gone down.*
　　　　　| *fallen.*

A *What about profit before tax?*
B *It hasn't changed.*

3 Complete this Chairman's Review. Put the verbs in brackets into the Present Perfect tense.

GRAPHIC IMAGES PLC

CHAIRMAN'S REVIEW OF ACTIVITIES AND OPERATIONS

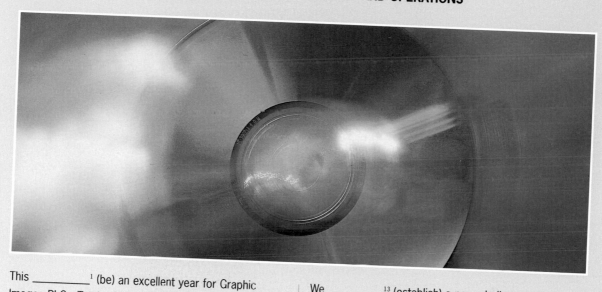

This _____¹ (be) an excellent year for Graphic Images PLC. Total sales _____² (reach) £370 million and sales within the UK _____³ (show) an impressive 8% growth. Export sales _____⁴ (fall) by 5% but gross profit _____⁵ (grow) by 3%. All business divisions _____⁶ (perform) well.

We _____⁷ (invest) heavily this year to improve quality. Our 'Quality Counts' programme _____⁸ (involve) many employees in individual and team projects and we _____⁹ (run) a series of training courses for technical personnel.

Our research and development work _____¹⁰ (continue) and we _____¹¹ (introduce) many new and enhanced products. We _____¹² (give) our customers increased support through our after-sales division.

We _____¹³ (establish) a new wholly-owned subsidiary, Graphic Finance Ltd., this year. So far this subsidiary _____¹⁴ (assist) over a thousand customers to lease Graphic Images equipment.

We _____¹⁵ (enter) two new partnerships this year. We _____¹⁶ (begin) a joint venture project with KARSTEL to develop an optical disk filing system and we _____¹⁷ (sign) a European distribution agreement with IND Amsterdam.

Kate Weston

Group Chairman

4 What about your company's recent activities and operations? Write down six things your company or department has done recently and tell a colleague about them.

Staff changes

1 These verbs are all connected with employment. Who does these things: employees (E), companies (C) or both (E/C)?

☐ resign   ☐ sack
☐ dismiss   ☐ recruit
☐ retire   ☐ make redundant
☐ take on   ☐ fire
☐ transfer   ☐ take early retirement

2 Use the correct form of each verb once to complete this personnel manager's report.

RESTRUCTURING

The plastics division has now moved from Royston to Harrow and we have achieved a 25% reduction in staff.

ROYSTON Reductions in staff		**HARROW** Increases in staff	
NATURAL WASTAGE			
Resigned	12	Employees transferring	30
Retired	4	New employees	20
Early retirement	8	Training scheme recruits	10
OTHER REDUCTIONS			
Redundancies	26		
Transferred	30		
Dismissed	-		
Total reduction	80	Total Increase	60

As far as possible, we have reduced the work force by natural wastage. We have not replaced workers who have _____¹ for personal reasons or _____² at the age of 60. Some workers have _____ _____ _____³ at 50 or 55, choosing to accept our generous package of financial incentives. Thirty workers have _____⁴ to the Harrow office.
One newspaper reported that we have _____⁵ or _____⁶ four workers in Royston for misconduct. This was untrue. We have not _____⁷ any workers this year. We have _____ 26 staff _____⁸ in Royston but we have _____ _____⁹ 20 new employees in Harrow. We have also _____¹⁰ 10 school leavers on the government's training scheme.

3 Ask and answer questions about the figures.

Ask about the employees.
How many workers have resigned?
Ask about the company.
How many staff have they made redundant?

4 Now ask your partner about recent staff changes in their company or department.

Has anyone retired recently?
Have you taken on any new staff recently?

Targets | **1** Study these sales results. Which regions

- have achieved their target?
- have exceeded their target?
- haven't achieved their target?

Region	Last year	This year	Target	Difference (%)
North	4,200	5,250	6,000	- 12.5
West	5,400	7,300	7,000	+ 4.3
East	4,110	5,500	5,500	0
Midlands	2,950	4,250	4,000	+ 6.25
South-West	2,950	4,600	4,600	0
South East	4,100	5,650	5,800	- 2.6

2 Question a partner about the figures.

A *How many units did they sell in the North last year?*
B *They sold 4,200.*
A *And how many have they sold this year?*
B *They've sold 5,250. They haven't achieved the target.*

3 You work for a pharmaceutical company. Your sales team sells two drugs: *Mevacin* and *Rovocor*. You want to give a prize to your best sales person. Work with a partner. Person A looks at the information below and Person B looks at the information on the next page.

Person A: Ask questions and complete the table. Then decide who this year's 'Top Sales Person' is.

AZTO PHARMACEUTICLALS
(Eastern Region) Sales Results

		Last year	This year	Target	Difference
Catherine Ceretta	Mevacin	2,900	4,100	4,250	- 3.6%
	Rovocor				
Carole Dubois	Mevacin	4,850	6,150	6,000	+2.5%
	Rovocor				
Peter Vogel	Mevacin	3,950	3,900	5,000	-22%
	Rovocor				

Person B: Ask questions and complete the table. Then decide who this year's 'Top Sales Person' is.

AZTO PHARMACEUTICLALS
(Eastern Region) Sales Results

		Last year	This year	Target	Difference
Catherine Ceretta	Mevacin				
	Rovocor	3,400	4,600	4,000	+15%
Carole Dubois	Mevacin				
	Rovocor	3,050	3,500	4,000	-12.5%
Peter Vogel	Mevacin				
	Rovocor	3,150	5,250	4,000	+31.25%

Checking progress

1 Work with a partner. Find out what they have done so far today. Have they

- spoken to anyone on the phone?
- written or received any letters or faxes?
- been to any meetings?
- travelled anywhere?
- had anything to eat?
- done anything else?

2 Look at the log on the opposite page and say what Ellen Roberts has done so far today.

She has written a letter to Paul Sykes and she's received ...

3 A colleague is asking Ellen about her progress. Act out their conversation with a partner.

Colleague How far have you got with Addington Bartlett? Have you written to Paul Sykes yet?

Ellen Yes, I have, but I haven't arranged an appointment yet. I'll do that next week.

4 [29] A few days later some people phone Ellen. Listen and work out who they are.

Hello, Ellen. I'm calling about those references. Have you had a chance to send them to me yet?
The caller is Michela Messina.

AREA REPRESENTATIVE'S LOG

| Sales rep. ELLEN ROBERTS | | Date 2ND NOVEMBER | Sheet No: 1 |

Company	Contact/tel. no.	Action taken	To do
ADDINGTON BARTLETT	PAUL SYKES 01436 852 407	LETTER SENT	ARRANGE AN APPOINTMENT NEXT WEEK
FOLEY INSTRUMENTS	SUNITA ADVANI 01799 524 888	LETTER RECEIVED	PREPARE A QUOTE ASAP
ANR TECHNOLOGIES	JORGE CASTANO 01767 313 705	PHONED	VISIT NEXT TUESDAY (SHOW SAMPLES)
TOWER SYSTEMS	ERICA WILLIAMS 01462 616 666	SALES LITERATURE SENT	TELEPHONE NEXT WEDNESDAY
OXFORD PUMP CO.	KATE COWE 01767 680 782	CALL RECEIVED	FAX A PRICE LIST ASAP
FORTEX	MICHELA MESSINA 01436 861 322	VISIT	WRITE A REPORT AND SEND REFERENCES NEXT WEEK
R + Q PLASTICS	CHRIS MURPHY 01799 986 329	MEETING	WAIT FOR HIM TO SEND SPECIFICATIONS

5 Practise making phone calls with a partner. One person should use the information below and the other should use the information in File 14 on page 160.

Call 1
You posted some goods to one of your customers yesterday. They phone you. Deal with the call.

Call 2
Your client was supposed to pay your invoice no. 6846 on the 14th. It's now the 25th and they still haven't paid. Phone them about it.

OBJECTIVE

to discuss future work
plans and schedules

TASKS

to talk about quantity:
how much and
how many

•

to predict events in
your company's future

•

to give strong advice
to colleagues

•

to follow a briefing on
a project schedule

•

to plan a new business
venture

PRESENTATION

I What security arrangements do you have in your place of work? How
do you prevent theft?

2 [32] Two managers discuss the security arrangements for their
company's new warehouse and distribution centre.

Listen to their conversation and decide which parts of the building
they are talking about. Mark the appropriate conversation number
on the plan opposite.

3 Now listen to each conversation again. Answer the questions and fill
in the spaces. Use one word per space.

[32a] How many windows will there be?

_____ _____ _____ in here?
_____ _____ _____ only one door?

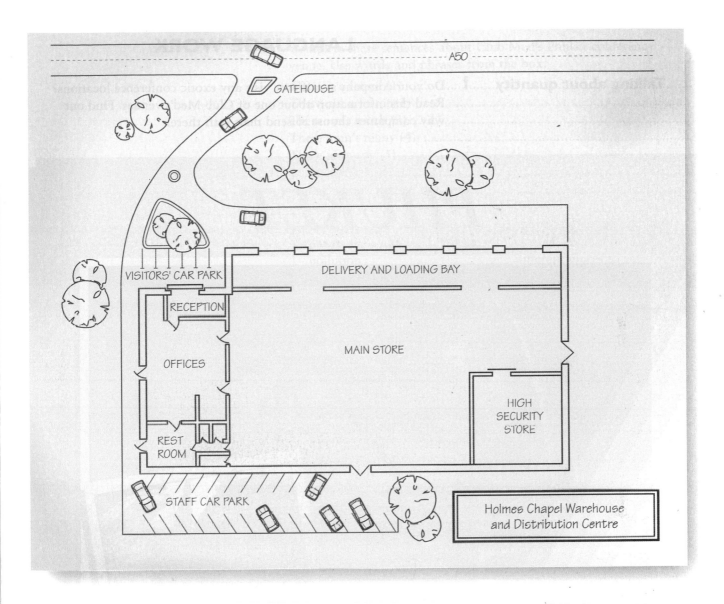

A50

GATEHOUSE

VISITORS' CAR PARK

DELIVERY AND LOADING BAY

RECEPTION

OFFICES

MAIN STORE

HIGH
SECURITY
STORE

REST
ROOM

STAFF CAR PARK

Holmes Chapel Warehouse
and Distribution Centre

32b What will the gatehouse workers do?
_____ _____ _____ will work here?
_____ _____ _____ will they need?

32c What will visitors do?
There _____ _____ _____ space,
_____ _____ ?
There _____ _____ _____ visitors.

32d Why will security be a problem?
This area _____ _____ very busy.
There _____ _____ doors.

32e Why are the doors a problem?
_____ _____ _____ have those doors there.
_____ _____ move the doors.

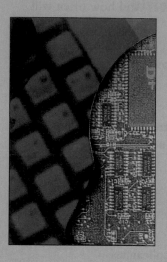

OBJECTIVE

to analyse and compare statistical information

TASKS

to complete a sales report

•

to contrast the economic performance of different countries

•

to choose between different suppliers

•

to compare stress and satisfaction levels in different occupations

PRESENTATION

1 Look at these statistics on sales of frozen foods. Which one is:

a   a bar graph
b   a table
c   a pie chart

Match these headings to the correct graph, table or chart.
1   Desserts – sales by value
2   Ready meals – sales by sector
3   Frozen foods – sales by sector

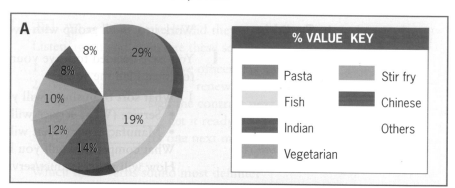

A

% VALUE KEY	
Pasta	Stir fry
Fish	Chinese
Indian	Others
Vegetarian	

29%, 19%, 14%, 12%, 10%, 8%, 8%

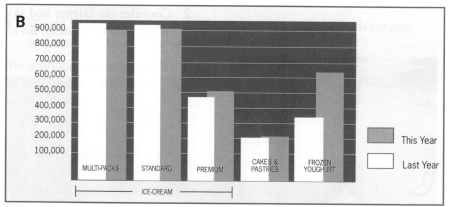

B

Bar graph with values 100,000–900,000 for: MULTI-PACKS, STANDARD, PREMIUM (ICE-CREAM), CAKES & PASTRIES, FROZEN YOUGHURT. This Year / Last Year

C

	Value £000	Volume (tonnes)
Meat and poultry	20000	7690
Vegetables	9200	8120
Fish	6000	1410
Ready meals	5300	1170
Desserts	2600	770
Pizzas	2300	330
Fruit	100	40
Totals	**45500**	**19530**

2 〔36〕 Listen to some retailers discussing the figures. You will hear three parts of their conversation. Match each part to the correct statistics.

3 〔36a〕 Listen to the first conversation again. Are these statements true (T) or false (F)? Correct the ones that are wrong.
1 Sales are lower than last year.
2 Ice-cream sales are higher.
3 Unusual flavours are popular.
4 Multi-packs were more popular in the past.

4 〔36b〕 Listen to the second conversation again.
1 Why are meat and poultry sales falling?
2 What is the fastest growing market?

5 〔36c〕 Listen to the third conversation again. Complete the missing words.
1 This is another fast growth market but it's _____ _____ than pizzas. We're offering a _____ _____ range and consumers are becoming _____ _____ .

2 But the market's becoming _____ _____ and the manufacturers have had to reduce their prices.
Are we getting _____ margins on these products now?
Yes, slightly.

6 *Cheap* and *expensive* are both adjectives. Notice how they are used in these sentences.

> Sales of cheap**er** ice-creams are falling.
> **More** expensive ice-creams are doing well.

We make comparative forms of adjectives with ...-**er** and **more**. When do we use ...-**er** and when do we use **more**?

7 *Popular* and *small* are both adjectives. Notice how they are used in these sentences.

> Pasta dishes are **the most** popular ready meals.
> Fruit is the small**est** sector of the frozen food market.

We make superlative forms of adjectives with **the most** and **the ...-est**. When do we use **the most** and when do we use **the ...-est**?

For more information on comparative and superlative forms, see page 172 in the Grammar and Usage Notes.

LANGUAGE WORK

Comparing sales figures

Complete this fashion retailer's report on sales. Use a comparative form of the adjective in brackets.

CLOVER RETAIL GROUP
NOVEMBER SALES REPORT

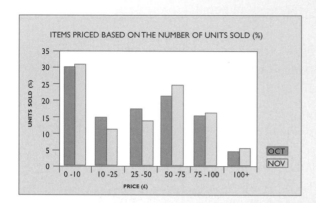

ITEMS PRICED BASED ON THE NUMBER OF UNITS SOLD (%)

We sold a _larger_ [1] (large) quantity of our _more expensive_ [2] (expensive) items this month (£50 and over). This was because we had a _____ [3] (wide) variety of suits and dresses in stock for the Christmas party season. _____ [4] (cheap) items (£10 and under) also did well but items in the mid-price ranges were _____ [5] (difficult) to move and sales were _____ [6] (low) than October.

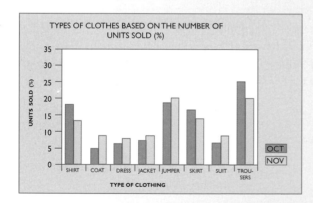

TYPES OF CLOTHES BASED ON THE NUMBER OF UNITS SOLD (%)

The _____ [7] (cold) weather led to an increase in coat sales. Jacket sales were also a little _____ [8] (high) than last month as were jumpers. _____ [9] (long) than average skirts did better than _____ [10] (short) ones and generally people preferred the _____ [11] (stylish) outfits. _____ [12] (casual) styles were less popular.

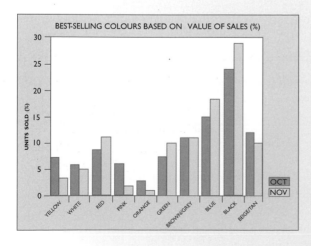

BEST-SELLING COLOURS BASED ON VALUE OF SALES (%)

There was a large increase in sales of _____ [13] (dark) colours such as black and navy blue. Red and green were _____ [14] (popular) than in October, but otherwise, the _____ [15] (colourful) items did badly. Yellows and pinks were much _____ [16] (slow) moving this month than last. Overall, sales in November were _____ [17] (good) than sales in October, but _____ [18] (bad) than last year when trading conditions were a lot _____ [19] (easy). We hope to see an improvement in December.

Comparing countries

1 Your company is planning to open new offices and factories around the world and you are collecting statistics. Study the graphs and complete the reports. Use only one word per space.

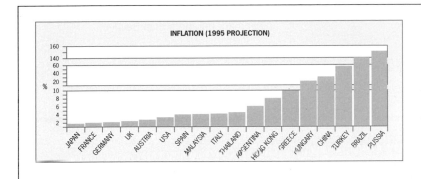

_____¹ has the highest rate of inflation and _____² has the lowest. The rate of inflation in _____³ is higher than Italy, but lower than in Argentina.

Source: The Economist Intelligence Unit

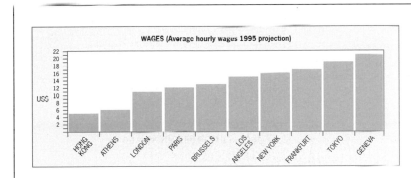

Workers in Geneva receive _____ _____⁴ wages and workers in Hong Kong receive _____ _____⁵. Parisians receive _____⁶ wages _____⁷ New Yorkers but _____⁸ wages _____⁹ Athenians.

Source: BICOI ; UBS

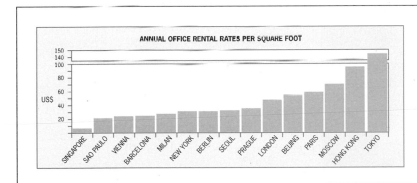

Companies in _____¹⁰ spend the most on rent and companies in _____¹¹ spend the least. Companies spend less on rent in _____¹² than New York but more than they spend in Barcelona.

Source: Moran Stahl & Boyer, 1994

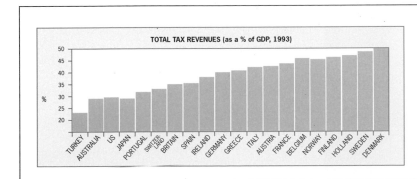

The Danes pay _____ _____¹³ tax and the Turks pay _____ _____¹⁴ . The Spanish pay _____ _____¹⁵ the Japanese but _____ _____¹⁶ the Italians.

Source: OECD

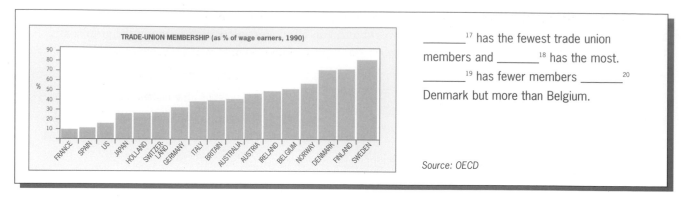

TRADE-UNION MEMBERSHIP (as % of wage earners, 1990)

_____ [17] has the fewest trade union members and _____ [18] has the most. _____ [19] has fewer members _____ [20] Denmark but more than Belgium.

Source: OECD

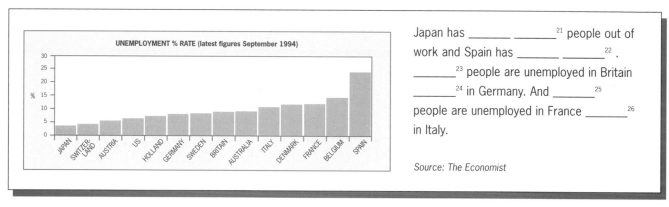

UNEMPLOYMENT % RATE (latest figures September 1994)

Japan has _____ _____ [21] people out of work and Spain has _____ _____ [22]. _____ [23] people are unemployed in Britain _____ [24] in Germany. And _____ [25] people are unemployed in France _____ [26] in Italy.

Source: The Economist

2 What about you? Where would you like to work? Which country in the world:

- has the highest living standards?
- has the nicest climate?
- has the most beautiful countryside?
- is the least polluted?
- is the safest?
- is the best place for children to grow up?
- is the best country to live in.

Why?

Comparing companies

1 Three companies produce the cardboard boxes you need. You are deciding which company to buy from. Your purchasing department has collected these statistics to help you make your minds up.

	EGP	The Card Company	Paper Packs Ltd
Price per standard 1 cubic metre box	7.56	7.4	7.83
No. of styles of boxes in the range	27	16	25
Quality – faults per 1,000 units	0.1	1.3	2.5
Delivery period	2 days	1 day	4 days
Discount	5%	10%	15%
Quantity kept in stock	100,000	600,000	500,000
Terms of payment	14 days	30 days	60 days

Work in pairs. Ask and answer the questions below.

Which company
1 has the highest/lowest prices?
2 has the widest/smallest product range?
3 has the best/worst quality record?
4 delivers the fastest/slowest?
5 gives the biggest/smallest discount?
6 keeps the most/fewest boxes in stock?
7 gives the most/least time to pay?

2 Cover up the questions. Look at the statistics and ask and answer the questions again.

3 Which supplier is best? Why?

4 Tell a colleague about your company's competitors.
1 Who are your main competitors?
2 Which company working in your field
• has the largest turnover?
• employs the most people?
• is the oldest?
• has the most branches/locations/products?
• provides the best service/product?

Why?

SKILLS WORK

Speaking 1

1 What things give you satisfaction in your job? Can you add anything to this list?

	Ranking
solving problems	
making money	
meeting people	
completing projects	
helping other people	
being part of a team	
having the power to make things happen	
having freedom to make decisions	
learning something new	
being creative	

Rank the different factors in terms of their importance to you. Give 1 to the most important, 2 to the second most important, and so on.

2 Compare your answers with your colleagues and explain your ranking.

3 Some jobs are more satisfying than others. Do these jobs give people more than an average degree of satisfaction or less? Decide with a partner, tick the boxes, then turn to File 26 on page 163.

	MORE SATISFYING THAN AVERAGE	LESS SATISFYING THAN AVERAGE
company director		
secretary		
primary school teacher		
probation officer		
computer programmer		
economist		
vet		
management trainee		
clergyman		
professional engineer		
shop assistant		
solicitor		

Reading   **1**   Look at the graphs in this article and say what you think it is about. Then read the article and find out if you were right.

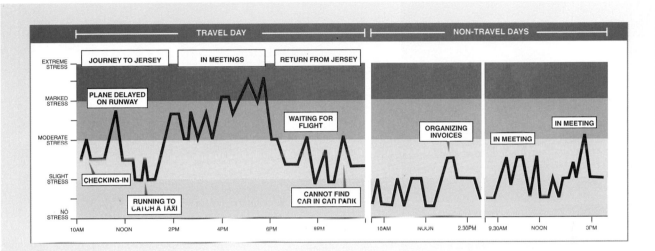

Which is better? An exciting job where you jump on planes and fly first class around the world or a quiet routine job where you only have to travel to the office and back. Recent research suggests many business people would prefer the second option. Psychologists working for British Telecom interviewed 75 senior managers last month, investigating complaints that too much travelling makes them irritable and depressed.

One psychologist followed a 36-year-old London jeweller about for three working days, monitoring and recording his stress levels. The first day was the worst. He went on a business trip to Jersey and his stress levels were twice as high as the following two days when he worked from his office. British Telecom is using the research to publicize its new range of teleconferencing machines – live videos that can connect people around the world via telephone lines.

2   What research did British Telecom do and why?

3   Which activities were more stressful for the jeweller:
   • meetings at home or meetings away?
   • checking in or running to catch a taxi?
   • waiting for a flight to take off or organizing invoices?

4   A jeweller is a person who makes or sells jewellery, such as rings or necklaces. Think of more jobs or professions that end with -er.

5   A psychologist is a person who studies the way people behave. Think of more professions that end with -ist.

6   The article mentions two symptoms of stress. What are they? Can you think of any more?

Speaking 2

I Lots of things can cause stress at work. Match these different causes and explanations.

1	Overcrowding	a	Too many bureaucratic procedures
2	Unrealistic deadlines	b	No spare money
3	Very tight budgets	c	Too little time to do the work
4	Downsizing	d	People not getting on with one another
5	Company reorganizations	e	Changing systems and job descriptions
6	Red tape	f	Physically threatening work conditions
7	Personality clashes	g	Too little space to work
8	Dangerous environments	h	Staff redundancies

Which of these problems do you face at work? Which do you find most stressful?

2 Some jobs are more stressful than others. How stressful are these jobs? Rank them. Give 1 to the most stressful and 10 to the least.

	my ranking	group ranking
museum worker		
miner		
computer operator		
shop assistant		
teacher		
personnel officer		
doctor		
civil servant		
advertising executive		
optician		

3 Compare your answers with some partners and decide on a group ranking. Then turn to File 18 on page 161.

Pronunciation

1 Practise saying some words from this unit and put them in the right stress pattern box.

psychologist	bureaucratic	operator	dangerous
procedure	redundancies	creative	personnel	engineer
satisfaction	retailer	unemployed	environment
advertising	assistant	occupation	consumer	economist

●••	
•●•	
••●	
●•••	
•●••	*psychologist*
••●•	

2 ⬜37 Listen and check your answers.

13

Business Travel

OBJECTIVE

to discuss changes to present arrangements

TASKS

to explain rules and regulations

•

to make travel enquiries

•

to discuss arrangements for a foreign visit

•

to propose and justify changes to a system in your workplace

•

to test your knowledge of international social customs

PRESENTATION

1 Do you like travelling by air? Why/why not?

2 Listen to three conversations at an airport. For each one, note down the traveller's problem and destination.

38a Problem ....
Destination ....

38b Problem ....
Destination ....

38c Problem ....
Destination ....

3 38a Listen to the first conversation again and supply the missing words below. Use one word per space.

1 _____ _____ get one in New York?
2 No _____ _____ _____ apply from outside the USA.
3 So _____ _____ get on this flight?

What will happen if the traveller goes to New York?

4 38b Listen to the second conversation again. What mustn't the traveller do? Why not? What doesn't she have to do? Why not?

5 38c Listen to the third conversation again and supply the missing words below.

1 If there's a seat in economy, _____ _____ _____ .
2 I'll see if _____ _____ _____ .
3 What happens if _____ _____?
4 We'll get you a seat with another airline if _____ _____
_____ .

6 Act out the third conversation with a partner. These words will help.

A afraid/overbooked
B last week
A very sorry
B must/Paris/10 o'clock. If/seat in economy/give
A afraid whole plane/full. Next flight/9.35/too late?
B No
A see/seat
B What/if not?
A seat with another airline/have to

LANGUAGE WORK

Air travel

"I have to ring my office."

"What's the taxi fare to the city centre?"

"Who won last night's ball game?"

"What's the code for Cleveland, Ohio?"

"Is it too early for the bar?"

"I have to be in Alaska by 8 tonight."

"Can I go through to the Departure Lounge now?"

"Is there anybody here to meet Mrs Leroy?"

"Where can I get a bus into town?"

"I can't find my boarding card."

"Do they take travellers' cheques at the Duty Free?"

"Where's the Gents?"

"How long is the stopover?"

"Will the flight leave on time?"

"Am I in time?"

"What star sign is the pilot?"

"I can't find a porter."

"Where are all the trolleys?"

"Can I leave my luggage here overnight?"

"Is this ticket out of date?"

"Where do I check in?"

"Where can I rent a car?"

"Can I reserve a hotel room in Denver, Colorado?"

"Which gate are we boarding from?"

"I have to catch the shuttle at 7."

"Do I have to declare my camera?"

"What's going on?"

"Can you cancel my hotel reservation?"

"I think that's my plane taking off."

"Please, somebody."

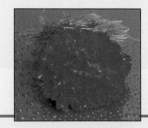

TWA HAVE THE ANSWERS.

We listened to travellers' questions at the airport and came up with an answer, in fact we came up with lots of answers – the TWA 'White Coats'.

'White Coats' are a team of young men and women at our Heathrow and JFK terminals – all available to help with your problems.

So the next time you're waiting for one of our six daily flights to the USA and your passport disappears or your colleague needs some elastic in a hurry, speak to the person in the white jacket with a red carnation in the buttonhole.

1   Which airline is this advertisement for?

What special service are they advertising?

2   Look at the left-hand column in the advertisement. Match the replies below to the correct problem.

1   No, it opened ten minutes ago.
2   No, but we've got a message for you.
3   There's an airport limousine downstairs.
4   The Cincinnati Reds.
5   Around £50.
6   Certainly. Go ahead.
7   I'll look up the best connection.
8   00 1 216.
9   When did you last have it?
10   There's a phone over there.

3   Look at the centre column in the advertisement. Find words or phrases that mean:

1   a person who flies planes
2   a person who carries luggage
3   a tax-free shop
4   a short stay in a place between connecting flights
5   baggage
6   things to carry baggage
7   the men's toilet
8   at the correct time
9   not late
10   expired (no longer useful or valid).

4   Look at the right-hand column in the advertisement. Find verbs or phrases that mean

1   getting on a plane
2   to tell a customs officer about something you are carrying
3   leaving the ground (a plane)
4   to book
5   the opposite of *to book*
6   the opposite of *to miss*
7   to hire
8   to register for a flight
9   happening
10   help!

5   Work with a partner. Take it in turns to be travellers asking the questions and a 'White Coat' answering them.

Rules and regulations

1 Study the table below then use each verb once to complete the regulations.

can	possible
can't/cannot	impossible
must	necessary or
have to	obligatory
don't have to	not necessary
mustn't	prohibited or forbidden

1 Passengers _____ make sure their luggage is clearly labelled.
2 Passengers _____ take a small bag onto the plane with them.
3 Passengers _____ carry dangerous articles such as compressed gases, weapons, explosives, or fireworks.
4 Passengers _____ check in 60 minutes before departure on international flights.
5 Passengers _____ check in 60 minutes before departure on domestic flights – 30 minutes is sufficient.
6 The airline _____ accept responsibility for delays due to bad weather.

2 Notice the difference between *mustn't* and *don't have to*. Decide which to use in these sentences.

1 They transfer our baggage to the next plane. We _____ carry it.
2 Passengers _____ use portable telephones because they interfere with the planes' electronic equipment.
3 Passengers _____ smoke when the plane is taking off or landing.
4 You _____ take out travel insurance, but it's a good idea.
5 This meeting is very important. We _____ be late.
6 We've got plenty of time. You _____ hurry.
7 You _____ return the car to the place you hired it. You can return it to another Hertz garage.
8 If you haven't got an international licence, you _____ drive.
9 You _____ pay to drive on motorways in England.
10 We can buy a ticket at the station. We _____ book in advance.

3 Compare your company's regulations and systems with a partner. Talk about the topics below. (Work with someone from a different organization if you can.)

travel expenses	retirement	holidays
lunch breaks	smoking	company cars
sickness	staff discounts	safety
hours of work	clothes/uniforms	security

Make sentences beginning:

We can …	*We can't …*	*We must …*
We have to …	*We mustn't …*	*We don't have to …*

Future possibilities **1** Match the two halves of these sentences.

1	If you keep the receipts, …	a	you must have a typhoid inoculation.
2	If I can't get a flight home, …	b	there are no hovercraft flights.
3	If it's 11 a.m. in London, …	c	we'll refund your travel expenses.
4	If they've caught the 2.30 from Paddington, …	d	she won't be able to change it.
5	If you haven't got anything to declare, …	e	how will you recognize him at the airport?
6	If you're travelling to Mozambique, …	f	you'd better hurry up.
7	If the sea is rough, …	g	she'll be on the next one.
8	If she bought a discount ticket, …	h	go through the green door.
9	If you're travelling from London to New York, …	i	they'll be here in half an hour.
10	If you have to be there by ten, …	j	put your watch back five hours.
11	If you haven't met before, …	k	it's 8 p.m. in Tokyo.
12	If she wasn't on that flight, …	l	I'll have to stay overnight.

For more information on conditionals see page 173.

2 You are going on a very important business trip to negotiate a large contract with a new supplier. What will you do if

- you miss your flight?
- you lose your luggage?
- your supplier is ill?
- your supplier can't speak English?
- your supplier invites you to lunch?
- your supplier's price is too high?
- your supplier offers you a bribe?

> *If I miss my flight,* *I'll catch the next one.*
> *I'll have to phone my supplier and explain.*

3 A client/colleague/customer is visiting your place of work next week. You are not sure how long they are staying or what they want to see. Write down some possible things to do. Think of

- people they could meet
- a guided tour of …
- processes to show them
- a presentation by … on …
- a place to have lunch
- an interesting place to visit nearby.

Work with a partner. Take it in turns to be the host(ess). Explain the different possibilities and find out what your visitor wants to do.

> *If you like,* *we can …*
> *If there's time,* *we could …*
> *If you're interested,* *we'll …*
> *If the weather's OK,*
> *If …*

Pronunciation

Voiced and unvoiced sounds

1 ⏮ 39 Listen to the first halves of some of the sentences below. Choose the correct ending then listen to the complete sentences and check your answers.

1 If you like, we can ride ... to the meeting in my new car.
   If you like, we can write ... a letter to the shareholders.

2 If the price ... is $500, we can't afford it.
   If the prize ... is a bottle of champagne, I'll share it with you.

3 If you change your glass, ... you can have some of this wine.
   If you change your class ... from business to economy, we can travel together.

4 If you want a view ... of the sea, we'll change your room.
   If you want a few ... moments to think, I'll leave you alone.

5 If we back ... your idea at the meeting, will you back ours?
   If we pack ... our suitcases now, we'll be ready to leave straight away.

2 Practise the sentences with a partner. One person should read a first half. The other should listen carefully and say the correct ending.

Company policy

1 Your company is reviewing its policies for business travel arrangements and expenses. Study the proposals below. What will happen if you implement them?

If staff travel economy class on flights, we can save a lot of money. If staff have to travel economy class, they won't like it.

GRAPHIC IMAGES PLC

PROPOSALS

1 Staff should travel economy class instead of business class on flights.
2 We should stop paying for alcoholic drinks at business lunches.
3 We should have a car pool instead of providing individual staff members with cars.
4 We should lease the company cars instead of buying them.
5 We should only buy/lease small cars (maximum engine size – 1,000 cc).
6 We should install meters in the company car park.

2 Hold a meeting with some colleagues to discuss the proposals. Decide which proposals to implement.

Social customs

1 Test your knowledge of social customs around the world. Do this quiz with a partner then check your answers in File 27 on page 163.

Culture Quiz

1 If you're doing business with a German, you have to shake hands
   a when you meet.
   b when you leave.
   c when you meet and when you leave.

2 In the Middle East you have to give presents to business contacts
   a in private.
   b in public.
   c every time you meet.

3 If you're giving a present to your Latin American customer, you mustn't give
   a cutlery.
   b food and drink.
   c a clock.

4 If an Indian says 'Come any time,' he or she expects you to
   a arrange a visit immediately.
   b visit him/her the next day.
   c ignore the invitation.

5 You can't do business in Muslim countries
   a on Wednesdays.
   b on Fridays.
   c on Sundays.

6 If an American nods his/her head, it probably means
   a I understand.
   b Yes.
   c I'm interested.

7 At a social occasion with an Indian client,
   a you can discuss business.
   b you mustn't discuss business.
   c you don't have to discuss business.

8 If you're doing business in Thailand, you must
   a shake hands firmly.
   b bow.
   c make sure you don't touch your head.

9 If a Japanese person gives you their business card, you have to
   a take it with both hands and study it carefully.
   b put it straight into your wallet or pocket.
   c write notes about them on it.

10 If you're in a pub in England, you have to buy a drink
   a for yourself.
   b for everyone in the group you're with.
   c for everyone in the pub.

Carnival. Rio de Janeiro, Brazil.

Beer Festival. Bavaria, Germany.

Chinese New Year, Singapore.

2 What about your country? Do you have any customs that sometimes surprise visitors from abroad?

SKILLS WORK

Reading | What customs surround a business lunch in your country?

1 What time do you eat?
2 How long does the meal last?
3 Do you talk about business all the time or just at the end of the meal?
4 Do you drink alcohol?

Compare your answers with this article.

Who's for a business lunch?

	TYPICAL LENGTH	USUAL TIME	BUSINESS TALK	ALCOHOL CONSUMPTION
UK	1 hour	1.00 – 2.00	throughout the meal	🍷🍷
Scandinavia	1 hour	12.00 – 1.00	throughout the meal	🍷
Russia	1.5 hours	1.00 – 2.30	throughout the meal	🍷🍷🍷
Germany	up to 2 hours	1.00 – 2.00	throughout the meal	🍷🍷🍷
Belgium/Netherlands	1 hour	12.00 – 1.00	throughout the meal	🍷🍷🍷
France/Luxembourg	2 hours	12.00 – 2.00	only after the cheese	🍷🍷🍷
Italy	2 hours	1.00 – 3.00 +	late in the meal	🍷🍷🍷🍷
Spain/Portugal	3 hours +	12.30 – 4.00	late in the meal	🍷🍷🍷
Greece	several hours	more likely to be dinner	occasionally	🍷🍷🍷🍷🍷

Forget the language barriers. Forget the jet lag. If you're travelling abroad on business, your most difficult problem is lunch. Every country has different customs and you can't afford to get it wrong.

Down in the south of Europe, lunch breaks last a long time. In Italy they can last three hours. In Spain they can be followed by a siesta. Some Greek people actually have a siesta instead of lunch, so they can prepare for a very substantial late dinner. And when dinner comes, everyone's attention is on the food. So don't worry if the business discussion is slow starting. The goal is to eat well, demonstrate hospitality and develop relationships. Business can wait.

Some lunches are lighter than others. If you're in Scandinavia, a business lunch is sometimes just a plate of sandwiches. And don't be surprised if your hosts refuse alcohol and drink milk instead – and skimmed milk at that. Not all places are so health conscious. As one Russian businessman remarked "The Americans are always complaining about smoking and drinking. In Russia we have no problem. We do both."

The French like to take a long time over their lunch. One traveller can recall a French lunch that lasted seven hours. French restaurants sometimes have a special 'business menu'. This is a trick. It's a reasonably quick three course meal designed for people who have no business to do. If you want to do business, choose from the real menu and take your time. Anything under about two hours is classed as a coffee break.

2 According to the writer, are these statements true or false?

	T	F
1 Lunch is a more serious problem than jet lag for business travellers.	☐	☐
2 People in Spain have a short sleep before lunch.	☐	☐
3 If you're dining with Greek people, they will talk about business all the time.	☐	☐
4 Scandinavians eat very substantial lunches.	☐	☐
5 Americans smoke and drink a lot at lunch.	☐	☐
6 French business menus are not suitable for people who have to do business.	☐	☐

Do you know any of the countries in the article? If so, do you agree with the writer? Which country's customs do you like most? Why?

3 Underline the odd one out in these lists of words. Then compare your answers with a partner. Do you agree?

lunch   dinner   <u>sandwich</u>   breakfast
A sandwich is a kind of food and the others are all meals.

1	Spain	Greek	France	Italy
2	milk	cheese	cow	butter
3	plate	knife	fork	spoon
4	coffee	tea	beer	water
5	skimmed	late	cold	fresh
6	beef	pork	lamb	pig
7	if	to	on	in
8	eat	drink	consume	have
9	strong	light	substantial	heavy
10	goal	target	objective	problem

Speaking Think of some changes you would like to make to a system at work. **Imagine changes to**

- methods of work
- communications procedures
- production systems
- the products/services that you provide
- your premises (the buildings you operate in)
- methods of supply or distribution
- any other process or arrangement that you can think of.

Argue the case for introducing changes.
1 Outline the present system or arrangement.
2 Explain the changes you want to make.
3 Explain why you want to make the changes. (What will happen if you do/don't?)
4 Answer questions from your colleagues.

OBJECTIVE

to show visitors
around a workplace

TASKS

to describe the
achievements of
companies and
individuals

•

to give an account of
your work experience

•

to explain systems and
processes

•

to write a report on
the benefits of a leasing
system

•

to follow a factory
tour

PRESENTATION

1 Do you ever show foreign visitors around your place of work? Who are the visitors and what do you show them?

2 Here are some photos of people at work. What do you think they are doing?

1

2

4

3

5

3 ⌷40⌷ Listen to some people showing visitors round. Match each conversation with the correct photographs.

4 Listen again and complete the missing words.

⌷40a⌷ The semi-conductors _____ _____ here.
Everyone _____ _____ from head to toe.

⌷40b⌷ _____ you _____ _____ an assembly line where the cars _____ _____ together?
It's the place where the cars _____ _____ apart.

⌷40c⌷ How long _____ he _____ here then?
_____ last year, I think.

⌷40d⌷ The testing _____ _____ in here.
_____ _____ $5 an hour.
_____ _____ _____ a local employment agency, but some of them have been coming here _____ years.

⌷40e⌷ _____ _____ have you been doing this?
Now everyone _____ _____ lifting techniques.
No one _____ _____ back problems _____ we started.

LANGUAGE WORK

Achievements

1 Have you ever heard of AMP? What do they produce and where are their products used?

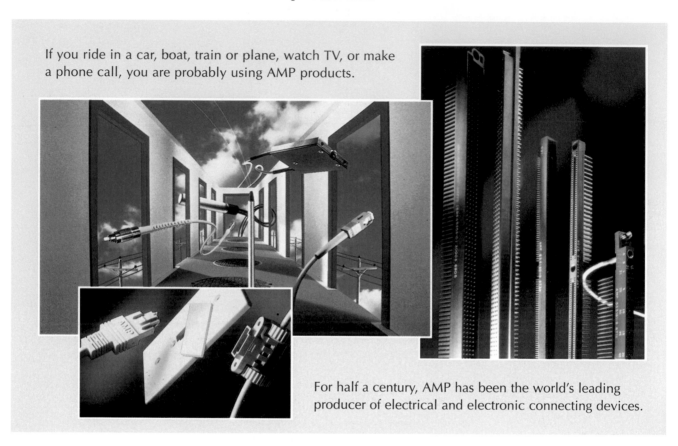

If you ride in a car, boat, train or plane, watch TV, or make a phone call, you are probably using AMP products.

For half a century, AMP has been the world's leading producer of electrical and electronic connecting devices.

2 Work with a partner. Look at these notes and ask and answer questions about AMP's past.

A *How long ago* | *did the company start trading?*
   When |

B *Over fifty years ago. / In 1941.*

THE **AMP** CORPORATION

1941	The company started trading.
1943	Invented the pre-insulated terminal that gave the company long-term leadership in the market.
1952	Set up its first foreign subsidiaries in Puerto Rico, France and Canada.
1959	Went public.*
1966	Joined the Fortune Magazine list of America's largest corporations.
1983	Opened a new corporate headquarters in Harrisburg, Pennsylvania.
1994	Achieved ISO 9000 quality certification throughout the corporation.

The company's stocks and shares were listed on the New York Stock Exchange.

3 All these actions happened in the past, but they connect to the present. For example, AMP still produce pre-insulated terminals and they still have subsidiaries abroad.

Work with a partner. Ask and answer questions about the present.

How long have AMP | *been in business?*
| *been producing pre-insulated terminals?*
| *had a subsidiary in Puerto Rico?*
| *been a public listed company?*
| *been in the Fortune Magazine list?*
| *been operating from their new headquarters?*
| *had ISO 9000 quality certification?*

GRAMMAR NOTE

There are two different forms of the Present Perfect tense, the continuous and the simple.
They've been producing | *pre-insulated terminals since 1943.*
They've produced |

In this situation the meaning is the same and English speakers usually use the continuous form, *They've been producing* ... However, with verbs like *be* and *have*, this is usually not possible.
~~They have been being in business since 1941.~~
~~They have been having a subsidiary in Puerto Rico since 1952.~~

---

4 We use *for* with a length of time and *since* with a point in time.
They've been in business for over fifty years.
They've been in business since 1941.

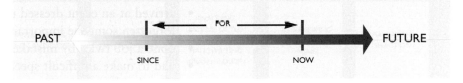

Decide whether to use *for* or *since* with the time expressions below.
1 ____ 2 days
2 ____ an hour
3 ____ Wednesday
4 ____ a long time
5 ____ last week
6 ____ 1945
7 ____ a month
8 ____ 2 o'clock
9 ____ years
10 ____ yesterday
11 ____ the 1960s
12 ____ the stock market crash.

3   Look at a factory manager's description of the process of making car bumpers. The steps are in the wrong order. Number them in the correct order.

We don't keep stocks of the finished bumpers. We operate a 'just in time' system.

☐ The computer arranges the production schedule.

☐ … before we pack them in crates.

☐ First we receive the order …

☐ … and we deliver them to the customers.

☐ … where we manufacture the bumpers.

☐ … and we feed it into the computer.

☐ We test the bumpers …

☐ Finally we load them into lorries …

☐ Next a conveyor belt takes the raw materials to the factory floor …

The whole process only takes about nine hours from start to finish.

[4I]   Listen to check your answers.

4   Now describe the process more formally, as shown below.
First an order is received and fed into …

Use these words to show the order of events.
First   Next   before   Finally

5   Draw a flow chart showing the steps and stages of a process in your workplace. You can choose any process you like. The ideas below may help you.

- developing a new product
- a manufacturing process
- a training process
- production planning
- ordering or buying goods
- an accounting process

6   Work in small groups. Take it in turns to give a short presentation to the group. Describe the order of steps in the flow chart and explain the process.

SKILLS WORK

Writing **1** You are examining the possibility of leasing your company's fleet of lorries. Read this advertisement for Lex Van Contracts. Which services are the most useful?

Lex Van Contracts take away the headaches of running the company fleet and allow you to get on with running the business.

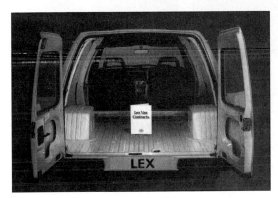

* We advise customers on the most cost-effective and efficient vehicles for their specific needs.
* We inspect every vehicle before delivery.
* We arrange signwriting.
* We replace tyres, batteries and exhausts when necessary.
* We service the vehicles at any time of the day or night.
* We provide a 24-hour recovery service.
* We deal with all the paperwork.
* We record the service history of our customers' fleets on our computer.

2 You decide to recommend Lex Van Contracts to your board. Write a report on all the services they offer. Use the Passive in your report.

MEMORANDUM

Date: ....

From: ...., Research Assistant

To: Helen Williams, General Manager

Subject: Fleet Leasing

As requested, I have been examining the possibility of leasing our fleet of lorries and I have found a suitable leasing company. Lex Van Contracts have an excellent reputation in the fleet leasing market. They provide a number of valuable services.

1 Customers are advised on the most cost-effective and efficient vehicles for their needs.

2 Every vehicle ....

3 Signwriting ....

4 Tyres, batteries, and exhausts ....

5 The vehicles ....

6 A 24-hour recovery service ....

7 All the paperwork ....

8 The service history ....

These services will offer substantial savings of administrative time and money. I therefore recommend we invite Lex to run the company fleet.

Listening

1 ⟨42⟩ You are going to hear a manager at Peugeot Talbot's car assembly plant showing some visitors round. While you listen, number the paragraphs in the right order.

☐ Fitting the windscreen

☐ Testing the brakes

☐ Hanging the doors

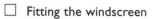

☐ Fitting the mechanical components

☐ Testing the car on the track

☐ Constructing the car body

☐ Fitting the wheels

☐ Painting the body

☐ Constructing the chassis

2 Now use the photographs to describe the process.

A *The car body is constructed.*
B *What happens* | *next?*
            | *then?*
            | *after that?*
A *The doors are hung.*

Pronunciation

[43] *Vowel sounds*

One word in each group has a different vowel sound to the rest. Listen and decide which word is different.

1	car	track	plant	last
2	step	eight	brakes	paint
3	wheel	each	test	me
4	door	bought	for	post
5	hung	come	one	worst
6	new	move	look	you

Speaking

Work in pairs or small groups. You are going to show a visitor around your organization.

1 First work out the scenario. Decide:

1 who the visitor is (potential client/supplier/sponsor, etc.)
2 what the purpose of the visit is
3 what you want to tell the visitor about your organization
4 which systems and processes they will be interested in
5 which parts of the building they should see
6 which people they should talk to.

2 Then plan an itinerary for the visit with times, places and people to meet. (Look at the itinerary on page 81 if you need help.)

3 Finally, act out the visit. The host(s) should make the visitor(s) welcome and take them to the places on the itinerary. The visitor(s) should ask questions about the things they see.

A visitor being shown round Glaxo's Zebulon plant.

OBJECTIVE

to discuss solutions to
business problems

TASKS

to consider the
consequences of
possible courses of
action

•

to explain problems
and suggest solutions

•

to look for
compromises in
conflict situations

•

to negotiate
agreements

PRESENTATION

1 🔊 What problem do you think these people have got? Listen and see if you are right.

2 Make a note of their problem in the chart below.

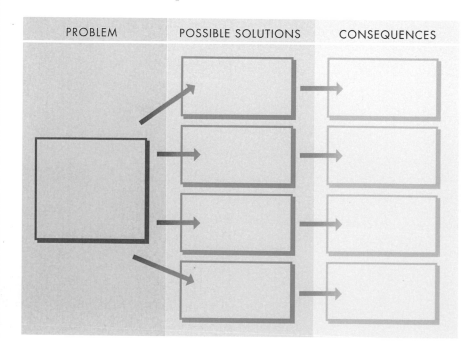

PROBLEM	POSSIBLE SOLUTIONS	CONSEQUENCES

3 ⌷44⌷ Listen again and make a note in the chart of all the possible solutions and consequences they discuss.

4 If they broke into the car, it would set off the alarm.

Use the chart to make more sentences with *If ...* .

5 What words are missing from these extracts? Can you remember? Write them in, then listen again to check your answers.

A Can you break into it?

B It _____ set off the alarm.

A We _____ phone and ask someone to bring them. Let's see. It's a fifty-minute drive. If they _____ now, they'd _____ here by two.

B That's too late. We _____ get to the airport in time.

B We could call the police. They _____ be able to open it.

A But they might _____. It'd be risky.

B _____ you took a taxi to the airport. It'd _____ one of us would be there to meet him.

6 Have you ever had a similar problem to this? What other travel problems have you had? How did you solve them?

LANGUAGE WORK

Consequences

1 Would you like to do any of these things?

- go on a training course
- buy a new computer or software package
- employ an assistant
- move to bigger premises
- speak better English
- have one more hour in the day

Explain why. Say what the consequences would be.
It would mean we/I could…
It would help us/me to…
It would enable us/me to…
It would save time because we/I could…
It would improve…

2 Are your problems getting on top of you? Are you feeling depressed and under stress? Read these suggestions. Which ones are good ideas? Underline the ones that could help you.

---

50 WAYS TO COPE WITH STRESS

Get up 15 minutes earlier. Prepare for the morning the night before. Don't rely on your memory … write things down. Repair things that don't work properly. MAKE DUPLICATE KEYS. **SAY "NO" MORE OFTEN.** **Set priorities in your life.** Avoid negative people. Always make copies of important papers. **ASK FOR HELP WITH JOBS YOU DISLIKE.** Break large tasks into bite sized portions. Look at problems as challenges. *Smile more.* **Be prepared for rain.** SCHEDULE A PLAY TIME INTO EVERY DAY. Avoid tight fitting clothes. Take a bubble bath. **BELIEVE IN YOU.** Visualize yourself winning. **Develop a sense of humour.** Stop thinking tomorrow will be a better today. Have goals for yourself. SAY HELLO TO A STRANGER. Look up at the stars. *PRACTISE BREATHING SLOWLY.* DO BRAND NEW THINGS. *Stop a bad habit.* TAKE STOCK OF YOUR ACHIEVEMENTS. **Do it today.** Strive for excellence, NOT perfection. LOOK AT A WORK OF ART. Maintain your weight. *Plant a tree.* *Stand up and stretch.* **Always have a plan B.** Learn a new doodle. **Learn to meet your own needs.** BECOME A BETTER LISTENER. *Know your limitations and let others know them too.* THROW A PAPER AIRPLANE. Exercise every day. **Get to work early.** CLEAN OUT ONE CLOSET. Take a different route to work. LEAVE WORK EARLY (WITH PERMISSION). **Remember you always have options.** Quit trying to "fix" other people. **GET ENOUGH SLEEP.** Praise other people. **RELAX, TAKE EACH DAY AT A TIME … YOU HAVE THE REST OF YOUR LIFE TO LIVE.**

---

3 Say what would happen if you did some of these things.

If I got up fifteen minutes earlier, I wouldn't be in a rush in the mornings.

If I prepared for the morning the night before, I'd sleep better at night.

Hypothesizing

We use *Supposing...* when we imagine hypothetical situations. Ask a partner what they would do in the situations below.

1 Supposing your boss wanted you to spend your summer vacation taking an English course. What would you do?
2 Supposing your company gave you a large sum of money to invest in your department. What would you spend it on?
3 Supposing someone offered you a job in Saudi Arabia at twice your present salary. Would you take the job?
4 Supposing the job were in the USA. What would you do?
5 Supposing you were made redundant. What would you do?
6 Supposing you wanted to start your own business. What sort of business would it be?

Problems

1 45 Listen to these workers' comments.

1 We can't get the staff we need.
2 Our suppliers are charging us a fortune.
3 Everything's going up – rent, heat, light, salaries ...
4 Our agents never get it right. Either they order too many or they order too few.
5 They're not interested in the work. They don't care whether they do a good job or not.
6 Our stocks are getting bigger and bigger.
7 If the management told us what they wanted, we'd know what to aim at.
8 The market's getting smaller day by day.

Match each comment to one of these problems. What problems are they complaining about?

a rising inventory costs
b poor staff motivation
c increasing overheads
d personnel shortages
e high materials costs
f unclear goals and strategies
g falling demand
h inaccurate sales forecasts

2 Are you facing any similar problems at work at the moment?

Solutions **1** Match the problems to the solutions and consequences.

PROBLEM	POSSIBLE SOLUTION	POSSIBLE CONSEQUENCE
We're having trouble with …	**We could …**	**But if we did, …**
1 one of our customers. They say they can't pay us until next year.	search people's bags when they leave the building.	we would have to pay higher prices.
2 the prototype for the new model.	look for other premises.	we might create bad feeling among the staff.
3 late deliveries from one of our suppliers.	dump some of the waste in the river.	our competitors might beat us to the market.
4 security. Someone is stealing small quantities of office supplies.	call in the receivers.	we wouldn't find anywhere as central and convenient as this.
5 the chemical treatment plant. It's not big enough.	take our custom elsewhere.	we'd only get a small part of the money they owe us.
6 our landlord. He wants to increase the office rents by 30%.	go back to stage one and redesign it.	would we poison the surrounding wild life?

2 Think of more possible solutions and consequences for the problems. Make sentences beginning *We could …* and *But if we did, …*

3 Think of another business problem, real or imaginary. Describe it to your colleagues and together, decide what to do about it.

Negotiating **1** With some business problems, you have to negotiate a solution and make compromises. Practise by negotiating a sale. First check you understand the terms below.

Price	$65 per piece
Credit period	30 days
Delivery time	8 weeks
Minimum order	500 pieces
Discount	5%
Cancellation penalty	50% if less than 4 weeks before delivery.

What problems might a customer have with these terms?
The price is rather high. The credit period is rather …

Work with a partner. Take it in turns to be the customer and supplier.
Customer *What's the price?*
Supplier *It's $65 per piece.*
Customer *That's rather high.*
Supplier *It compares favourably with our competitors.*

These phrases will help the supplier to justify his or her position.

It compares favourably with our competitors.	
I'm afraid	it's customary.
	it always takes that long.
	it's company policy.
	we always insist on this.

2 Now take it in turns to suggest alternatives.

Customer *We didn't expect the price to be so high.*
Supplier *What did you have in mind then?*
Customer *$60 per piece.*
Supplier *I'm afraid we couldn't accept that.*

3 The customer wants the supplier to:

- give them a discount for bulk purchase.
  (10% on orders over 1,000 pieces)
- provide an early settlement discount.
  (2% for settlement within 14 days)
- deliver earlier.
  (the end of next month)
- accept a penalty clause for late delivery.
  (10% price reduction for each month of delay)
- supply good support documentation.
  (a full set of manuals, free of charge)
- extend the one-year warranty period.
  (to two years)

Work with a partner again. Practise suggesting compromises.

Customer *We'd like you to give us a discount for bulk purchase.*
Supplier *Could you be more specific?*
Customer *Yes, we'd like a 10% discount on orders over 1,000.*
Supplier *That's rather difficult, but 8% might be possible.*

4 The supplier wants the customer to:

- make their payment in dollars
- pay a 20% deposit immediately
- pay the balance within 30 days
- accept a penalty clause for cancellation
- place regular monthly orders of at least 750 pieces
- recommend them to other potential clients.

Look at Exercise 3 again and suggest more compromises.

Supplier *We'd like you to make your payment in dollars.*
Customer *If we paid in dollars, would you give us a discount for bulk purchase?*
Supplier *Yes, we could accept that. / No, I'm afraid that's not possible.*

FILE 13
SEE PAGE 44

1 Check your answers below.

1	write, right	6	two, too, to
2	meet, meat	7	four, for
3	would, wood	8	there, their, they're
4	no, know	9	buy, by, bye
5	hear, here		

2 Good dictionaries contain phonetic spellings. They can help you to pronounce words. Here are the phonetic spellings for the words in exercise 1, but they are in a different order. Match them with the right words.

a /nəʊ/ _no, know_

b /fɔːr/ _____

c /raɪt/ _____

d /hɪər/ _____

e /miːt/ _____

f /ðeər/ _____

g /tuː/ _____

h /wʊd/ _____

i /baɪ/ _____

3 What words are represented by these phonetic spellings? (Look at exercise 2 for help.)

1	/gəʊ/	5	/fiːt/
2	/mɔːr/	6	/weər/
3	/waɪt/	7	/huː/
4	/bɪər/	8	/gʊdbaɪ/

12b Listen and check your answers

FILE 14
SEE PAGE 105

Call 1

You placed an urgent order with your supplier a week ago. They promised to deliver within five days. The goods still haven't arrived. Phone your supplier and complain.

Call 2

You sent your supplier a cheque this morning to pay invoice no. 6846. Your supplier calls you. Deal with the call.

FILE 15
SEE PAGE 52

You are the public relations officer of Facit – a Swedish office equipment company. A newspaper reporter is writing an article on your company. Use these notes on the company history to answer their questions.

1413	Facit starts trading in Sweden as a small copper mining company.
1889	Facit begins manufacturing furniture.
1928	Facit establishes its first subsidiary in Denmark.
1938	Facit buys the company *Halda Typewriters*.
1938	Facit introduces its products into the USA.
1950	Facit establishes subsidiaries in the USA and Brazil.
1956	Facit builds the first Swedish computer.
1979	The Facit 2254 calculator becomes standard in Tokyo's largest bank.
1985	Facit launches its first laser printer.
1990	Facit opens a marketing co-ordination centre in Brussels.
1994	Facit establishes new distribution channels in Europe.

FILE 16
SEE PAGE 47

PROGOLF

Just the thing to keep the golf fan happy on rainy days.

ProGolf is an advanced microchip electronic golf game for one or two players. Each player has a set of 12 golf clubs to choose from as they go round the course, complete with bunkers and lakes. Perfect speed and timing are necessary to win and the game is a sensation with serious (and not so serious) golfers.

Comes with full instructions and batteries.
A colour booklet provides a map of each hole.

18cm x 8cm x 2cm.   **Weight 180g**   **£49.95**

FILE 17

SEE PAGE 143

1 Complete these questions with the correct form of *make* or *do*.

1 Are you _____ any progress with that report?
2 Has that newspaper article _____ any damage to our reputation?
3 Did we _____ a profit on that deal?
4 If you have time, could you _____ some research for me?
5 Have you ever _____ a complaint in a restaurant?

2 Now ask your partner the questions and listen carefully to their answers. Do they make sense?

3 Your partner will ask you some questions. You should answer them with one of these sentences. Be careful. They are not in the correct order.

- No, this is the first time we've ever had anything to do with them.
- No, I think we've made a big mistake.
- Certainly. I'll do it straight away.
- It depends. What do you want me to do?
- Yes, I'm calling the States. We're doing a job out there.

FILE 18

SEE PAGE 127

3 This is how a Consumers' Association report ranked the jobs for stress. Do you agree?

THE DEGREE OF STRESS ASSOCIATED WITH DIFFERENT OCCUPATIONS	
miner advertising executive doctor teacher personnel officer shop assistant civil servant optician computer operator museum worker	most stressful ↑ ↓ least stressful

FILE 19

SEE PAGE 85

Here is your diary for next week. Your partner calls you.

9 MONDAY	2 p.m. Berenice Jardine Space Utilization Services
10 TUESDAY	10 a.m. – 6 p.m. Industrial Lubricants Trade Fair, Harrogate
11 WEDNESDAY	08.10 Fly to Luxembourg LG 402 (Return 20.30 BA 149)
12 THURSDAY	1.00 pm. Lunch, J. Coleman Brewster, L'Assiette au Beurre
13 FRIDAY	2.00 p.m. Pollution Control meeting
14 SATURDAY	7.30 p.m. London Symphony Orchestra, Royal Festival Hall
15 SUNDAY	

FILE 20

SEE PAGE 54

Try to remember what Flora said. Write in the words.

Flora _____

Roger Hello, Flora. How are you?

Flora _____

Roger Fine. What can I do for you, Flora?

Flora _____

Roger Oh dear. How many did we deliver?

Flora _____

Roger I'm sorry about that. I'll send the rest immediately.

Flora _____

Roger Yes, of course. Is there anything else?

Flora _____

16b Now listen again and check your answers.

FILE 21 SEE FILE 10

1   *Cancellation* and *postponement*.

2   sth stands for something.

3   US marks an American spelling.

4   /ˈkænsl/ and /pəˈspəʊn/ help you to pronounce the words.

5   ☛ directs you to a note about a similar word.

6   ☆ tells you cancel is an important word to learn.

FILE 22 SEE PAGE 107

You are a stock broker. A client calls to find out how their shares have performed this week. Here is your client's portfolio and this morning's newspaper headlines. Tell them today's prices and give them advice about what shares to buy more of and what shares to sell.

	Holding (no. of shares)	Last week's price (p)	Today's price (p)
Nitro Chemicals	500	186	200
Forsythe Bank	500	246	301
Webb Communications	1,000	167	167
Bespoke Tailoring	1,500	427	431
Rose Computers	2,000	174	154
Pharmedico Drugs	2,500	466	423

Forsythe Bank computer fraud: employee steals £5m

AIDS CURE BREAKTHROUGH AT PHARMEDICO

Bespoke tailoring wins Queen's Award for Industry

When you have finished, turn to File 12 for next week's share prices.

FILE 23 SEE PAGE 93

1 Listen to your partner's description of the turnover of a company over a period of twelve months and complete the graph below.

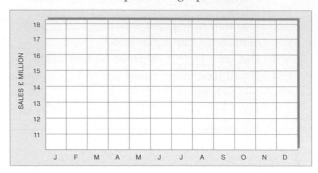

2 The graph below shows the energy costs of a company over a period of twelve months. Describe it to your partner.

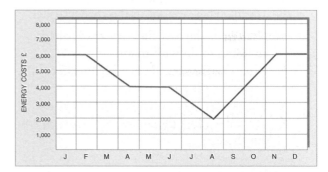

FILE 24 SEE PAGE 47

OFF THE WALL TENNIS BALL ALARM CLOCK

Just the thing to help you get up on Monday morning.

It's seven o'clock in the morning and your alarm clock starts to ring. But you've got 'Off the Wall'. You reach over, pick it up and throw it against the wall. It falls silent. You get up feeling better. What a wonderful way to start the day!

'Off the wall' is a 10cm diameter shock proof electronic alarm clock. It comes complete with its own stand.

(Batteries are not supplied) £9.95

FILE 25

SEE PAGE 143

1 Complete these questions with the correct form of *make* or *do*.

1 Could you _____ me a favour?
2 Would you phone round some suppliers and _____ enquiries?
3 Have you ever _____ business with that company before?
4 Are you _____ a long distance call?
5 Do you think we've _____ the right decision?

2 Your partner will ask you some questions. You should answer them with one of these sentences. Be careful. They are not in the correct order.

• No, I'm afraid we made a loss.
• No, I've never had to do that. Have you?
• Yes, but there's nothing we can do about it now.
• Yes, it's nearly finished. Are there any more to do?
• I'll do my best but I can't make any promises.

3 Now ask your partner the questions from exercise 1. Listen carefully to their answers. Do they make sense?

FILE 26

SEE PAGE 124

3 Compare your answers with these survey results. Does anything surprise you?

HOW PEOPLE IN DIFFERENT OCCUPATIONS RATE THEIR DEGREE OF JOB SATISFACTION	
MORE THAN AVERAGELY SATISFIED	LESS THAN AVERAGELY SATISFIED
clergyman	economist
company director	computer programmer
solicitor	professional engineer
primary school teacher	secretary
insurance broker	management trainee
probation officer	shop assistant

Taken from a Consumers' Association Report

FILE 27

SEE PAGE 135

Answers

1 You have to shake hands when you're coming or going in Germany, but in Britain you usually only shake hands when you meet someone for the first time.
2 You have to give your present in public in the Middle East to show it's not a bribe, but it's good manners to give your present in private in Asia.
3 You mustn't give cutlery in Latin America because it suggests that you want to cut off the relationship. You mustn't give food or drink in Saudi Arabia because it suggests you think your hosts aren't offering you enough to eat and drink. You mustn't give a clock in China because the Chinese word for clock is similar to the word for funeral.
4 'Come any time' means 'I want you to visit me' in India. If you don't suggest a time and arrange a visit immediately, an Indian will think you are refusing the invitation. But if an English person says 'Come any time', they will think you are bad-mannered if you start fixing a date.
5 Offices are usually closed on Fridays in Muslim countries.
6 Americans usually mean 'Yes' when they nod their heads. An English person probably just means 'I understand', and an Asian is just showing interest.
7 It's bad manners to discuss business at a social occasion in India.
8 In Thailand you have to shake hands very gently. It's not like America where a weak handshake can indicate a weak character. In Japan you have to bow when you meet someone for the first time but in Thailand you have to put the palms of your hands together in a prayer gesture. And you mustn't touch your head in Thailand. It's bad manners.
9 You must treat your contact's business cards with respect in Japan. You have to study them before you put them away and you mustn't write on them.
10 In an English pub, you have to take your turn to buy a 'round' – a drink for everyone in your group.

FILE 28

SEE PAGE 142

You all work for an executive recruitment agency. You are looking for good managers to fill top jobs. Interview the people in the other group and collect information to add to your database. Use this form.

PR PROFESSIONAL RECRUITMENT

PERSONAL DETAILS

Name	
Company	
Education & Qualifications	
Languages	

EXPERIENCE

		YEARS
Present job		
Previous jobs		

FILE 30

SEE PAGE 47

LANGUAGE TRANSLATOR

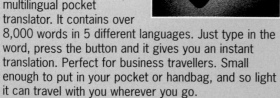

Just the thing to take with you on your next foreign business trip.

Here is the world's first multilingual pocket translator. It contains over 8,000 words in 5 different languages. Just type in the word, press the button and it gives you an instant translation. Perfect for business travellers. Small enough to put in your pocket or handbag, and so light it can travel with you wherever you go.

The memory contains more than 1,600 words in each language.

14cm x 6cm   weight 100g (batteries not supplied) £34.95

FILE 29

SEE PAGE 87

You are expecting a visitor from your parent company for three days next week. The visitor wants to meet the people on this list. You contacted them to find out when they are free.

Mrs Carne –   Free any day before 12

Mr Gandhi –   Free all day Tuesday, and Wednesday afternoon

Miss Carley – Free any time on Monday or Wednesday. Away all day Tuesday.

Mr Barnes –   Away all day Monday. Free any time on Tuesday or Wednesday.

Ms Lyon –   Free 1–3 p.m. Tuesday, and all day Wednesday.

The visitor phones you. Help to arrange their schedule.
Write in the times.

The visitor calls you again with a problem. Help him/her to change the schedule. Change the schedule.

21	MONDAY	9-10	a.m.
		10-11	a.m.
		11-12	a.m.
		12-1	p.m.
		1-2	p.m.
		2-3	p.m.
		3-4	p.m.
		4-5	p.m.
22	TUESDAY	9-10	a.m.
		10-11	a.m.
		11-12	a.m.
		12-1	p.m.
		1-2	p.m.
		2-3	p.m.
		3-4	p.m.
		4-5	p.m.
23	WEDNESDAY	9-10	a.m.
		10-11	a.m.
		11-12	a.m.
		12-1	p.m.
		1-2	p.m.
		2-3	p.m.
		3-4	p.m.
		4-5	p.m.

Grammar and Usage Notes

I THE PRESENT SIMPLE TENSE

USES	EXAMPLES	UNIT
Permanent or long-term situations	She **lives** in New York. Who do you **work** for? We **produce** and **sell** computers.	1, 3
Facts	It **weighs** 2570 kg. How long **does** it **take**? What does 'convenient' **mean**?	4
Regular activities and routines	They **travel** to work by train. I usually **read** the *Financial Times*. How often **do** you **play** golf?	6
Feelings	I **prefer** white wine. I **don't like** horror films.	6
Opinions and states of mind	I **don't agree.** How **do** you **feel** about this?	7
Timetables and schedules	When **does** the London train **leave**? The board meeting **starts** at 3.30 p.m. It **doesn't finish** till 8.30.	8

FORMATION

■ Add an *s* to the 3rd person singular form.

I You They	leave	at 8 a.m.
He She It	leaves	

■ Use *do* as a help verb to make question forms.

Do	I you we they	leave at 8 a.m.?
Does	he she it	

■ Use *do* as a help verb to make negative forms.

I You We They	**don't**	leave at 8 a.m.
He She It	**doesn't**	

■ Use *do* as a help verb in short answers.

Do you work for BICC?
Yes, I do.

Does she work for BICC too?
No, she doesn't.

2 THE PRESENT CONTINUOUS TENSE

USES	EXAMPLES	UNIT
Actions happening now	We're **introducing** new systems. I'm **waiting** for Miss Rowntree. Who's **calling** please?	3
Future plans and arrangements	When **is** he **arriving?** She's **meeting** the CEO at 2 p.m. **Are** you **doing** anything special tonight?	8

FORMATION

■ Use the verb *be* and *-ing*.

I am	(not) working today.
You are	
He is	
She is	
It is	
We are	
They are	

■ Don't forget to use contractions.

I'm	I'm not
You're	You aren't
He's	He isn't
She's	She isn't
It's	It isn't
We're	We aren't
They're	They aren't

■ Change the word order to form a question.

Am I	working today?
Are you	
Is he	
Is she	
Is it	
Are we	
Are they	

3 THE PAST SIMPLE TENSE

USES	EXAMPLES	UNIT
Finished past actions	I **joined** the company in 1989. What **happened**? It **didn't sell** well in the Middle East. What quantity **did** we **deliver**? How long ago **did** they **start** trading?	5, 9, 14

FORMATION

■ With regular verbs, add *-ed* to make the Past Simple form.

Nissan open**ed** the Yokohama plant in 1936.
We launch**ed** our first laser printer in 1985.
The meeting start**ed** late.

■ Irregular verbs have a special past form*.

to go   I **went** to a trade fair in Barcelona.
to rise   Inflation **rose** last month.

■ Use *did* as a help verb to make negatives, questions, and short answers.

The meeting **didn't** start on time.

What time **did** you arrive?

Did you go to the trade fair last month?
Yes, I **did**. Did you?
No, I **didn't**.

*See page 177 for a table of common irregular verbs.

4 THE PRESENT PERFECT TENSE

We use the Present Perfect tense to talk about past actions with present importance.

1 FINISHED ACTIONS

USES	EXAMPLES	UNIT
Past actions with results in the present	Graphic Images **has had** excellent results this year. We **haven't achieved** our target. **Have** you **finished** yet?	10
Life experiences	I've **forgotten** his name twice. **Have** you ever **missed** a flight? I've never **been** to Italy.	14

2 UNFINISHED ACTIONS †

USES	EXAMPLES	UNIT
Past actions that are continuing now	He's **been** working there for 5 years. They've **had** a subsidiary here since 1952. How long **have** they **been** in business?	14

† See page 141 for more information on for *and* since, *and on the Simple and Continuous forms.*

Notice we use the past tense when a definite time is understood.

A   We've opened a new factory in Roubaix.
B   When **did** you **do** that?
A   Last January.

A   Have you ever been to China?
B   Yes, I have. I **visited** Beijing in 1987.

A   I've cancelled the order.
B   Why **did** you **do** that?

Americans sometimes use the Past Simple where the British use the Present Perfect.

American English   Did you phone her yet?
British English   Have you phoned her yet?

FORMATION

PRESENT PERFECT SIMPLE

■ Use *have* as a help verb in all forms. Use it with the third part of the verb.

I You We They	have haven't	broken the machine.
He She It	has hasn't	

■ Change the word order to form a question.

Have	I you we they	broken the machine?
Has	he she it	

■ Use the help verb in short answers.

Have you spoken to the Legal department?
No, I **haven't**, but my colleague **has**.

PRESENT PERFECT CONTINUOUS

■ Use *have* as a help verb in all forms. Use it with *been* and *-ing*.

I You We They	have haven't	**been** working for an hour.
He She It	has hasn't	

■ Change the word order to form a question.

Have	I you we they	been working for an hour?
Has	he she it	

■ Use the help verb in short answers.

Has he been working here long?
No, he **hasn't**. Has she?
Yes, she **has**. She's been working here for ten years.

5 FUTURE TIME

USES	EXAMPLES	UNIT
Timetables and schedules	The Board meeting **starts** at 3.30 p.m. When **does** the London train **leave**?	8
Plans and arrangements	When **is** he **arriving**? She's **meeting** the CEO at 2 p.m. **Are** you **doing** anything special tonight?	8
Intentions	We're **going to** open a new sales office in Spain. Who **are** you **going to** invite to the meeting?	7 7
Instant decisions	Hold on. **I'll** get a pencil. She's busy. — Then **I'll** come back later.	2
Future facts and predictions	**We'll** need a big hotel. How many people **will** work here? There **won't** be much space.	11

6 MODAL VERBS

Modal verbs are special help verbs. They add extra meaning to the main verb.
Most modals have more than one use.

VERBS	EXAMPLES	USES	UNIT
Can	**Can** I use your phone? **Can** you quote me a price for CIF New York? Passengers **can** take a small bag onto the plane with them. I **can't** find my boarding card.	permission requests possibility/ability inability	2, 13
Could	**Could** I interrupt a moment? **Could** you speak up? We **could** ask for volunteers.	permission requests suggestions	2, 7
May	**May** I borrow your car?	permission	2
Might	It **might** be possible to reduce the price.	future possibility	15
Will	**I'll** tell him to phone you back. How many people **will** work here? There **won't** be much space.	promises future facts predictions	2, 11
Would	**Would** you speak more slowly please? What **would** you like to drink? **Would** you like to come to a party? I'd love to. What time **would** suit you? **Would** you reduce the price, if we paid cash?	requests offers invitations suggestions suggestions	2, 6, 8, 15

Shall	**Shall** we ask for volunteers? **Shall** I call a taxi for you? What **shall** I do?	suggestions offers asking what to do	7, 11
Should	I think we **should** teach the French sales staff English. The government **should** increase taxes on petrol.	recommending action saying what is right or correct	7
Must	Passengers **must** make sure their bags are clearly labelled. Passengers **mustn't** carry guns or explosives.	obligation prohibition	13

FORMATION

Use the modal verb with the stem of the main verb.

> She can speak Russian.
> This product will sell well.

Make a question by changing the word order.

> Can she speak Russian?
> Will this product sell well?

Make a negative by adding *not* to the modal verb.

can't	mustn't	couldn't
cannot	shouldn't	wouldn't

But be careful. There are some exceptions

1 *Will not* is very strong. *Won't* is more common in spoken English.

2 *Mightn't*, *mayn't*, and *shan't* are unusual.

Don't add *-s* in the 3rd person singular.

~~She can speaks Russian.~~
~~This product will sells well in the Far East.~~

Don't use *do* as a help verb to make negatives and questions with modal verbs.

~~I don't can swim.~~
~~Do you can swim?~~

Don't use *to* after modal verbs.

~~We must to increase our productivity.~~

7 COMPARATIVES AND SUPERLATIVES

USES	EXAMPLES	UNITS
Comparing two things	This month's sales are **higher than** last month's. The market is getting **more competitive**. English cars aren't **as reliable as** German cars.	12
Comparing three or more things	It's **the cheapest** product in the range. Which city is **the most expensive** to live in?	12

FORMATION

SHORT ADJECTIVES

■ Add -*er* or -*est* to adjectives with one syllable.

high	higher	highest
cheap	cheaper	cheapest
big	bigger	biggest

LONG ADJECTIVES

■ Use *more* or *most* with adjectives with two or more syllables.

modern	more modern	most modern
expensive	more expensive	most expensive
competitive	more competitive	most competitive

■ Watch out for these two irregular forms.

good	better	best
bad	worse	worst

■ Add -*er* or -*est* to adjectives with two syllables ending in -*y*.

easy	easier	easiest

MUCH

■ Use *much* to make the comparative adjective stronger.

It's **much** more expensive.
The climate is **much** better in France than Scotland.

8 CONDITIONALS

USES	EXAMPLES	UNITS
Possible situations	If there's a seat in economy, give me that. If it's 11 a.m. in London, it's 8 p.m. in Tokyo. If she bought a discount ticket, she won't be able to change it.	13
Hypothetical situations	If I were offered a job abroad, I'd take it. If we agreed to 5 per cent, would you give us 60 days' credit?	15

FORMATION

◾ In most conditional sentences, use the tenses that are natural for the situation. But be careful. It's very unusual to use *will* in the same clause as *if*. After *if*, use a present tense to express a future idea.

If you **buy** 500, we'll give you a discount.

◾ In hypothetical situations, use a past form to express a future idea. This suggests something is less likely to happen.

If you **bought** 500, we'd give you a discount.

◾ You can put the *if* clause at the beginning or end of the sentence.

If I see him, I'll tell him.
I'll tell him, if I see him.

If you paid cash, we'd give you a discount.
We'd give you a discount, if you paid cash.

9 THE PASSIVE

USES	EXAMPLES	UNITS
Describing actions – without saying who does them	The company's activities **are divided** into six business areas. **It's made** of paper. Nissan UK **was founded** in 1969.	3, 4, 5
Describing processes	The data **is fed** into the computer. The bumpers **are packed**, and taken to the lorries.	15

FORMATION

◾ Use the verb *be* as a help verb. Use it with the third part of the main verb (the past participle)

Then the	component is compenents **are**	**taken** to the factory floor.

◾ To change the tense, change the form of the verb *be*.

It	**is** **was**	made by hand

10 COUNTABLE AND UNCOUNTABLE NOUNS

English nouns are divided into two groups: countable nouns and uncountable (mass) nouns. *Machine* and *job* are countable nouns. *Machinery* and *work* are uncountable nouns. For more examples of countable and uncountable nouns see Units 6 and 12.

■ Countable nouns are singular or plural.

machine	machines
job	jobs

Uncountable nouns are never plural.

machinery
work

■ Countable nouns have singular or plural verb forms.

That machine **breaks** down every week.
Those machines **break** down every week.

The job **is** very interesting.
The jobs **are** very interesting.

Uncountable nouns never have plural verb forms.

That machinery **breaks** down every week.
The work **is** very interesting.

■ Singular nouns can have *a* or *an* in front of them.

We need **a** new machine.
It's **an** interesting job.

Uncountable nouns never have *a* or *an* in front of them.

We need (some) new machinery.
It's interesting work.

■ Use *many* with countable nouns.

How **many** new machines do we need?
There aren't **many** jobs left to do.

Use *much* with uncountable nouns.

How **much** new machinery do we need?
There isn't **much** work left to do.

II NUMBERS

CARDINALS AND ORDINALS

Cardinal		Ordinal		Cardinal		Ordinal	
1	one	1st	first	16	sixteen	16th	sixteenth
2	two	2nd	second	17	seventeen	17th	seventeenth
3	three	3rd	third	18	eighteen	18th	eighteenth
4	four	4th	fourth	19	nineteen	19th	nineteenth
5	five	5th	fifth	20	twenty	20th	twentieth
6	six	6th	sixth	21	twenty-one	21st	twenty-first
7	seven	7th	seventh	22	twenty-two	22nd	twenty-second
8	eight	8th	eighth	30	thirty	30th	thirtieth
9	nine	9th	ninth	40	forty	40th	fortieth
10	ten	10th	tenth	50	fifty	50th	fiftieth
11	eleven	11th	eleventh	60	sixty	60th	sixtieth
12	twelve	12th	twelfth	70	seventy	70th	seventieth
13	thirteen	13th	thirteenth	80	eighty	80th	eightieth
14	fourteen	14th	fourteenth	90	ninety	90th	ninetieth
15	fifteen	15th	fifteenth	100	a hundred	100th	hundredth

LARGE NUMBERS

1,000	a thousand
1,000,000	a million
1,000,000,000	a billion (American English)
1,000,000,000,000	a billion (British English)

■ *In the past, American and British billions were not the same. But British companies and newspapers often use American billions now.*

FRACTIONS

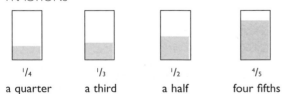

1/4	1/3	1/2	4/5
a quarter	a third	a half	four fifths

MONEY

■ Write money signs in front of the numbers. But pronounce currencies after the numbers.

$56	fifty-six dollars
£200	two hundred pounds
¥5,000	five thousand yen

DECIMALS

■ Write the decimal point sign as a dot, not a comma.

0.5	nought point five
0.25	nought point two five

■ Pronounce numbers individually after a decimal point.

10.06	ten point oh six
27.27	twenty-seven point two seven

■ 0 is pronounced *nought* before a decimal point and *oh* after a point in British English.

0.05	nought point oh five

■ It can be pronounced *zero* in American English.

0.05	point zero five

12 TIME

DAYS

Monday	Friday
Tuesday	Saturday
Wednesday	Sunday
Thursday	

MONTHS

January	July
February	August
March	September
April	October
May	November
June	December

SEASONS

spring
summer
autumn*
winter

(American English: fall)

YEARS

Written English	1066	1999
Spoken English	ten sixty-six	nineteen ninety-nine

DATES

	British English	*American English*
Written English	16(th) September 16/9/98	16(th) September 9/16/98
Spoken English	The sixteenth of September September the sixteenth	Sixteenth September September sixteenth

TELLING THE TIME

■ A simple way to tell the time is to say the numbers.

10.20 ten twenty   11.15 eleven fifteen   4.45   four forty-five

■ You can say the hours in two ways:

nine   nine o'clock

■ But don't make this common mistake:

~~nine-thirty o'clock~~

■ You can also tell the time this way:

one o'clock

ten past three

a quarter past four

half past five

twenty-five to six

a quarter to seven

■ In American English you can use different prepositions.

Ten past three or Ten after three
Quarter to seven or Quarter of seven

■ British and American speakers do not usually use the twenty-four-hour clock.

11.00 eleven o'clock
23.00 eleven o'clock

To be more exact they say:

eleven a.m. or eleven in the morning and
eleven p.m. or eleven at night

■ But they do use the twenty-four-hour clock to talk about train and plane timetables.

19.30 The train leaves at nineteen thirty.

13 IRREGULAR VERBS

STEM	PAST TENSE	PAST PARTICIPLE	STEM	PAST TENSE	PAST PARTICIPLE
be	was/were	been	let	let	let
become	became	become	lie	lay	lain
begin	began	begun	lose	lost	lost
break	broke	broken	make	made	made
bring	brought	brought	mean	meant	meant
build	built	built	meet	met	met
buy	bought	bought	pay	paid	paid
catch	caught	caught	put	put	put
choose	chose	chosen	quit	quit	quit
come	came	come	read	read	read
cost	cost	cost	ride	rode	ridden
cut	cut	cut	ring	rang	rung
deal	dealt	dealt	rise	rose	risen
do	did	done	run	ran	run
draw	drew	drawn	say	said	said
drink	drank	drunk	see	saw	seen
drive	drove	driven	sell	sold	sold
eat	ate	eaten	send	sent	sent
fall	fell	fallen	set	set	set
feed	fed	fed	shake	shook	shaken
feel	felt	felt	shoot	shot	shot
fight	fought	fought	show	showed	shown
find	found	found	shut	shut	shut
fly	flew	flown	sing	sang	sung
forbid	forbade	forbidden	sink	sank	sunk
forget	forgot	forgotten	sit	sat	sat
freeze	froze	frozen	sleep	slept	slept
get	got	got *	speak	spoke	spoken
give	gave	given	spend	spent	spent
go	went	gone	split	split	split
grow	grew	grown	spread	spread	spread
have	had	had	stand	stood	stood
hear	heard	heard	steal	stole	stole
hide	hid	hidden	stick	stuck	stuck
hit	hit	hit	swim	swam	swum
hold	held	held	take	took	taken
hurt	hurt	hurt	teach	taught	taught
keep	kept	kept	tear	tore	torn
know	knew	known	tell	told	told
lay	laid	laid	think	thought	thought
lead	led	led	throw	threw	thrown
learn	learnt	learnt	understand	understood	understood
leave	left	left	wear	wore	worn
lend	lent	lent	win	won	won
			withdraw	withdrew	withdrawn
			write	wrote	written

American English: gotten

11

I need a thing to show transparencies.
And have you got a thing to write on?
I also need a thing to turn the video on.
And I need a thing to make my voice louder.

Do you have a thing to hold my slides?
Ah! I need a thing to put my papers on when I'm speaking.
Sorry to trouble you again, but I also need a thing to write with.
Just one more thing. Do you have a thing to put the plug in?

12a

1	write	6	two
2	meet	7	four
3	would	8	there
4	no	9	buy
5	hear		

12b

1	go	5	feet
2	more	6	wear
3	white	7	who
4	beer	8	good bye

13

Good morning, everyone. Today I'd like to introduce you to the new product in the range next season – a new version of the aerobic cycle – the AC5.

As you know, the previous model, the AC4, was very successful last year. It's popular with sports centres and commercial users, but it doesn't sell well in the domestic sector of the market.

The AC5, on the other hand, is designed for the domestic user. It's lightweight, only eleven kilograms, so it's easy to pick up and carry about. It's only 38 cm wide and 65 cm long, but it has the same high stability as all our other aerobic cycles.

It has most of the usual features too: modern design, comfortable padded handlebar grips, and safety footstraps. It comes with a liquid crystal display meter, to measure speed and distance. The handlebars move from 75 to 102 cm and the seat is height adjustable. So the AC5 is suitable for every member of the family.

But the special feature of the AC5 is that it's collapsible. When not in use, it folds up for easy storage. This will be a strong selling point in the domestic market.

5 REPORTING

14

A This project has a long history, John. Could you fill me in on the background?
B Yes, the idea for the product is very old. It was around in 1989 when I joined the company, but we didn't run a feasibility study until 1991.
A Were the results positive?
B Yes, very positive, and we started designing the prototype at the beginning of 1992. We constructed it that summer and ran tests in the autumn. We had some technical problems at that stage.
A Did you solve them?
B Yes, but it took a long time. We didn't finish till June 1993.
A What happened then?
B We prepared detailed drawings.
A How long did that take?
B Six months. Then we sent them to potential customers. There were lots of things the customers didn't like. We began modifying the designs at the end of '93. It took twelve months.
A Why did it take so long?
B We were very short-staffed, and we had problems with the computer.
A What problems?
B That was the year we lost a lot of data on Friday the thirteenth.
A Yes, I remember.
B We were ready to manufacture in Spring 1995, but by then there were a lot of similar products on the market. We couldn't make a profit on the line.
A So you had to shelve the project?
B That's right.

15a

We prepared designs and discussed them with the clients before we started. We looked at the drawings together and they liked them. We provided detailed specifications and showed them the plans at every stage. They discovered a few small mistakes but we corrected them. We changed anything they didn't like. We even included extra features when they asked for them. Then as soon as we finished they complained and said they wanted something different.

15b

prepared	corrected
discussed	changed
started	included
liked	asked
provided	finished
showed	complained
discovered	wanted

16a

Hello Roger. It's Flora Silveira.
I'm fine, thanks. And you?
I'm afraid there's a problem with our order. You delivered the wrong quantity. 60. We asked for 80.
Thanks a lot. Can you send them today.
No, that's all thanks.

16b

A Hello, Roger. It's Flora Silveira.
B Hello, Flora. How are you?
A I'm fine, thanks. And you?
B Fine. What can I do for you, Flora?
A I'm afraid there's a problem with our order. You delivered the wrong quantity.
B Oh dear. How many did we deliver?
A 60. We asked for 80.
B I'm sorry about that. I'll send the rest immediately.
A Thanks a lot. Can you send them today?
B Yes, of course. Is there anything else?
A No, that's all thanks.

6 SOCIALIZING

17a In the office

A Paolo! It's great to see you again. Do come in. Shall I take you coat?

B Thanks.

A Have a seat. Did you have any trouble finding the way?

B No. Your directions were very good.

A How long did it take?

B Only an hour.

A Would you like some coffee?

B Yes please, I'd love some.

A And how is Stephania?

B Oh, she's fine. She sends her regards, by the way.

A Milk?

B No, black please.

A Here you are.

B Thanks.

17b In the car

B It's strange driving on the left-hand side of the road.

A Yes. Is this your first visit to Cambridge?

B Yes, it is. I'd love to see the university.

A Then let me show you round tomorrow.

B Oh, would you? That's very kind of you. Is there a good golf course in Cambridge?

A I think so, but I don't play myself.

B Are you interested in sport?

A No. Not really. What about you?

B I like golf and I go skiing about once a month in winter.

A Where do you go. In Italy?

B Yes. A small place near Chatillon. It's in the Alps.

17c In the restaurant.

C The wine list, sir.

A Thank you. Let's see. What sort of wine do you like, Paolo?

B I prefer white.

A Sweet or dry?

B Dry.

A Then let's have the Chablis. It's usually very good.

B How often do you come here?

A About once a month.

(*to the waiter*) Excuse me.

C Yes sir?

A We'll have the Chablis, please. Number sixty-three.

B And I'd like a bottle of mineral water too, please.

18

A I'd like a cheese sandwich, a chicken sandwich, and a cherry tart served with chocolate sauce.

B OK. So that's a cheese sandwich, a chicken sandwich, and a cherry tart served with chocolate sauce.

A Ah, sorry. Can I change the cherry tart served with chocolate sauce?

B Certainly.

A I'll have fresh English strawberries served with sugar and sweet champagne.

B OK. So that's fresh English strawberries served with sugar and sweet champagne.

7 MEETINGS

19

A The next item on the agenda is the new Spanish sales organization. As you know, we're going to open the new sales office in March and so we need to discuss recruitment. Basically we have two alternatives. We can either take on new Spanish sales representatives and train them. Or we can teach our French sales reps Spanish and transfer them. Any views on this, Marcel?

B Yes. The important thing here is product knowledge, not language. The French sales staff have already got the product knowledge. They know how the company operates too. I think we should teach them Spanish and transfer them.

A How do you feel about that proposal, Carlos?

C I don't agree. It takes years to learn a language. But why don't we employ Spanish staff, and send them to France for technical training?

B No. It's a waste of time, if they can't speak French.

C What do you think, Nancy?

A I don't know. how long does it take to train a new sales rep, Marcel?

B It depends on the rep. Usually about a year.

A Mmm. That is a problem. But I think nationality is important here. It's a Spanish branch so I don't think we should employ French nationals. Now I know you're not going to agree with me here, Marcel, but as I see it we have no choice...

20

1 We're going to work ...
   We're going to work together in a joint venture.

2 We're going to sit ...
   We're going to sit down and start the meeting now.

3 We're going to have ...
   We're going to have a long discussion.

4 We're going to lock ...
   We're going to lock the door.

5 We're going to leave ...
   We're going to leave at five o'clock.

21a

A Right. Shall we move on to the next item on the agenda? This is a proposal to print a special catalogue for our multimedia products. What's everyone's reaction to this?

B It's a terrific idea. Right now they're all mixed up with everything else in the main catalogue. Nobody notices them.

C I agree. But how much is it going to cost? I'd like to see some figures.

A OK. So we need to work out the costs. Could you deal with that, Thierry?

B Sure.

A How soon can you prepare some figures? By Friday?

B Yes, OK.

A Excellent. We can discuss this again next Monday, then.

encyclopedia around in their head.

And that's all from the business news studio today. We'll be back tomorrow at five past one.

31				
1	stock	for	drop	from
2	share	their	where	year
3	by	height	half	price
4	make	head	blame	chain
5	close	were	term	first
6	warm	short	point	fall

11 PLANNING

32a

A What will you keep in here?

B A lot of electronic stock – high value items.

A Will there be only one door?

B Yes, and there won't be any windows.

A Good.

32b

A How many people will work here?

B Two. One to check the traffic coming in and one to check the traffic going out.

A How much equipment will they need?

B Just a telephone line to the main building.

32c

B All visitors will report here first.

A Good. There won't be much space, will there?

B Well, there won't be many visitors. We'll only need a desk for the receptionist and three or four chairs.

32d

B This area will be very busy. A lot of trucks will come in and out of here each day.

A And there are six doors. Security will be a problem.

B I know.

A You'd better install closed circuit television cameras.

32e

A You'd better not have those doors there. They open straight onto the car park. It'll be easy to take things from the main store and drive off.

B I know. People will walk out the back of the building and we won't see them.

A You'd better move the doors.

B I can't. It's the fire regulations.

A What will you do about security then?

B We'll fit alarms. They'll go off every time the doors open.

33

1 He'll call you when he's got the information.

2 We've been very busy so I haven't had much time today.

3 I'm not in the office next week but I'd like to arrange a meeting with you the week after.

4 You'd better not sign the contract until they've checked it.

5 She doesn't know what it's like.

34

a

A I don't know when I'll get time to get to the post office.

B Shall I post them for you?

A Oh, that'd be great. Thanks a lot.

B You're welcome.

b

C It's no good. The battery's flat.

D Shall I give you a push?

C Could you? That's very kind of you.

c

E Oh no!

F Here, shall I open the door for you?

E Yes, please.

F You've got a lot there. Shall I give you a hand?

E No, It's all right thanks. I can manage.

d

G What a nuisance! My hands are wet.

H Shall I answer it for you?

G Yes please, if you could.

e

J Oh, damn! It's my best suit as well.

K Shall I get you a cloth?

J No, it's all right thanks. I can manage.

f

L Number 25. Well that's it. I've lost all my money.

M Shall I buy you a drink?

L No, thanks all the same.

M Well, shall I give you a lift home, then?

L Yeah, I think you'd better.

35a

A Could you tell me the schedule?

B Yes, of course. As you know, we plan to move offices this autumn.

A What about the building you're in now? When does the lease run out?

B In October. We don't intend to renew it.

A So where will the new offices be?

B The Business Park. We expect to sign the contract next week. It's a nice modern building. We aim to get it ready by the end of September. I can't give you an exact moving date yet but I hope to fix one next month.

A How big is it?

B 2,200 square metres.

A But that's tiny. How will everyone fit in? There won't be enough space.

B Only half the staff will be there.

A What do you mean?

B A lot of the staff will become teleworkers. They'll work from home.

35b

A I don't like the idea.

B Why not? There are lots of advantages. We'll be able to save on rent and reduce our overheads.

A It won't work. The staff need access to office equipment.

B They'll all have computers. And they'll come into the office for monthly meetings.

A They won't like it. They'll miss the human interaction.

B Nonsense. They'll enjoy working at home. There'll be no more commuting in rush hour traffic.

A But how will you check they're working? How will you motivate them?

B They'll be in daily contact with their supervisor - by phone.

A But they won't be able to learn from their colleagues.

B Lots of companies are employing teleworkers these days....

12 COMPARING INFORMATION

36a

A What are the figures like?

B Well... sales are about the same as last year. The biggest sector of this market is ice-cream and we've sold less than last year.

A That's bad news.

B Yes, but the more unusual flavours are doing well. We've sold more premium brands but fewer standard.

A What about multi-packs? How are they doing?

B They aren't as popular as they were. But look at the figures for yoghurt.

A Hey, they're good!

36b

A How do these figures compare with last year's?

B People are eating less meat so sales are down there.

A Do we know why?

B The market is getting smaller. It's part of a general trend towards healthier diets.

A Are we selling more vegetables?

B Yes, but the fastest growing sector here is pizzas. They're sixteen per cent up on last year.

36c

B This is another fast growth market but it's more mature than pizzas. We're offering a much wider range and consumers are becoming more adventurous. Almost half our sales are international recipes now; Italian, Chinese, Indian.

A What about curries?

B Yes, spicy dishes like curries are doing well. But the market's becoming more competitive and the manufacturers have had to reduce their prices.

A Are we getting lower margins on these products now?

B Yes, slightly.

37

psychologist   satis<u>fac</u>tion

<u>bu</u>reau<u>cra</u>tic   <u>re</u>tailer

<u>o</u>perator   unem<u>ploy</u>ed

<u>dan</u>gerous   en<u>vi</u>ronment

pro<u>ce</u>dure   <u>ad</u>vertising

re<u>dun</u>dancies   as<u>sis</u>tant

cre<u>a</u>tive   occu<u>pa</u>tion

perso<u>nnel</u>   con<u>su</u>mer

engi<u>neer</u>   e<u>co</u>nomist

13 BUSINESS TRAVEL

38a

A Is there a problem?

B Yes. I'm sorry, but your US entry visa has expired.

A Can I get one in New York?

B No. You have to apply from outside the USA.

A So I can't get on this flight?

B I'm afraid not. If we take you to New York, the immigration authorities won't let you in.

38b

A I got in from Toronto late and I've missed my connection to Newcastle.

B If there's space, you can have a seat on the next flight.

A Good, but I mustn't be in the smoking section. I'm allergic to smoke.

B That's all right.

A What about my luggage?

B You don't have to do anything about that. We'll transfer it to the plane for you.

A Thanks.

38c

A I'm afraid it's overbooked.

B But I booked last week.

A I'm very sorry.

B Look. I must be in Paris by ten. If there's a seat in economy, give me that.

A I'm afraid the whole plane's full. The next flight doesn't arrive till 9.35. Is that too late?

B No, it's all right.

A I'll see if there's a seat.

B What happens if there isn't?

A Don't worry. We'll get you a seat with another airline if we have to.

39

1 If you like, we can write ...
    If you like we can write a letter to the shareholders.

2 If the prize ...
    If the prize is a bottle of champagne, I'll share it with you.

3 If you change your glass ...
    If you change your glass, you can have some of this wine.

4 If you want a view ...
    If you want a view of the sea, we'll change your room.

5 If we pack ...
    If we pack our suitcases now, we'll be ready to leave straight away.

14 COMPANY VISITS

40a

A The semiconductors are manufactured here. Come and look through the window.

B What are they all wearing?

A It's a clean room. Everyone is covered from head to toe.

B To stop dirt getting on the components?

A Yes, dust and dirt. I'm afraid we can't go in.

B That's OK.

40b

A Have you ever seen an assembly line where the cars are put together?

B Yes?

A Well this is the dis-assembly line.

B Dis-assembly?

A Yeah. It's the place where the cars are taken apart.

B But why?

A To learn about recycling. We've been studying how to reuse the parts.

40c

A Who is that?

B Reg Parks. He works in the maintenance department.

A Is he tuning it?

B No. He likes to come in here in his lunch breaks and play the pianos. He couldn't play a note when he started working here. He's quite good now.

A How long has he been here, then?

B Since last year, I think.

40d

A The testing is done in here.

B That's amazing. Do these people do this all day?

A Yes. They're paid $5 an hour. We don't employ them directly. They're supplied by a local employment agency, but some of them have been coming here for years.

B How far do they walk?

A About 14 miles a day. 20,000 steps is the same as several years of carpet wear.

40e

A What's happening?

B It's an exercise session. We have them every morning.

A How long have you been doing this?

B For the last four years. Before that, the employees used to get a lot of injuries, back problems mostly, from all the heavy lifting they have to do. Now everyone is taught lifting techniques.

A Does it work?

B Yes. No one has had back problems since we started.

41

We don't keep stocks of the finished bumpers. We operate a 'just in time' system. First, we receive the order and we feed it into the computer. The computer arranges the production schedule. Next, a conveyor belt takes the raw materials to the factory floor where we manufacture the bumpers. We test the bumpers before we pack them in crates. Finally, we load them into lorries and we deliver them to the customers. The whole process only takes nine hours from start to finish.

42

This is the body construction plant, where the process starts. First the chassis are constructed. Then the car bodies. After that the doors are hung. If you come over here, you can see the new door-hanging equipment in operation. Electronic sensors are used to position the doors accurately.

The next stage in the process is treatment and painting. Would you like to follow me into the paint plant?

The painting process is rather interesting. Each car is electrically charged so it attracts the paint like a magnet. This gives a better finish and reduces waste. Shall we move on?

This is the final assembly area. The next step is to fit the car windows and the windscreen.

The cars are now ready for the mechanical components. The engine, the gear box, and the suspension units are fitted here. Then, after that, the wheels are fitted. Over there you can see our new rolling road test equipment. A sophisticated computer programme is used to test the brakes.

And here, outside the plant, is the evaluation track. Every new car is driven round this track before the final quality checks. It's about one kilometre long and it's designed to test the car over a lot of different road conditions.

43

1	car	track	plant	last
2	step	eight	brakes	paint
3	wheel	each	test	me
4	door	bought	for	post
5	hung	come	one	worst
6	new	move	look	you

15 TACKLING PROBLEMS

44

A I'm afraid we've got a problem.

B What's that?

A I've locked the keys in the car.

B Oh no!

A What time does Mr Lee's flight arrive?

B Three o'clock. I've said we'll be at the airport to meet him. Can you break into it?

A It would set off the alarm.

B Is there a spare set of keys?

A Yes, but they're back at the office.

B We could phone and ask someone to bring them. Let's see. It's a fifty-minute drive. If they left now, they'd be here by two.

A That's too late. We wouldn't get to the airport in time.

B OK. Let's think about this.

A I know. We could call the police. They might be able to open it.

B But they might not. It'd be risky.

A Supposing you took a taxi to the airport. It'd mean one of us would be there to meet him.

B And you could wait here for someone to bring the spare keys, then come and pick us up later.

A Yes.

B OK then. I'll call a taxi. Can I use your mobile phone?

A Ah!

B What's the matter?

A It's in the car.

45

1 We can't get the staff we need.

2 Our suppliers are charging us a fortune.

3 Everything's going up – rent, heat, light, salaries …

4 Our agents never get it right. Either they order too many or they order too few.

5   They're not interested in the work. They don't care whether they do a good job or not.
6   Our stocks are getting bigger and bigger.
7   If the management told us what they wanted, we'd know what to aim at.
8   The market's getting smaller day by day.

46a

A   We need better information about the market and we'd like your help.
B   What did you have in mind?
A   We'd like you to send us your sales statistics every week instead of every month.
B   That's rather difficult. It takes a long time to compile those statistics.
A   I know, but they're very important.
B   If we sent you the statistics every week, would you pay our costs?
A   Could you be more specific?
B   Would you pay for an extra day's secretarial help?
A   It might be possible. One day, you say?
B   Yes.
A   OK. We could accept that.

46b

B   We didn't expect these sales targets to be so high.
A   They're based on last year's sales. We followed the standard formula.
B   But last year's sales were unusually high. We had a large order from the Ministry of Defence.
    Supposing you subtracted that order from last year's figures. You could set a target based on ...
A   No. I'm sorry. We couldn't accept that. The targets must be based on the total figure. It's company policy. We always insist on this.

46c

A   Is that everything?
B   Yes, I think so.
A   Could we go through it again and check what we've agreed?
B   Yes, of course.

A   Right. You're going to send us your sales figures every week.
B   That's right. And you're going to pay for four days' secretarial help each month.
A   No. We agreed to pay for one day.
B   But you said you wanted the figures every week.
A   But it won't take you four days to prepare them.

47

1   I didn't say we would pay you five hundred **pounds**.
2   **I** didn't say we would pay you five hundred pounds.
3   I didn't say we would **pay** you five hundred pounds.
4   **I** didn't say we would pay you five hundred pounds.
5   I didn't say we **would** pay you five hundred pounds.
6   I didn't say we would pay you **five** hundred pounds.
7   I didn't say we would pay **you** five hundred pounds.

© Oxford University Press
Great Clarendon Street, Oxford OX2 6DP

Oxford   New York

Athens Auckland Bangkok Bogota Buenos Aires
Calcutta Cape Town Chennai Dar es Salaam
Delhi Florence Hong Kong Istanbul Karachi
Kuala Lumpur Madrid Melbourne Mexico City
Mumbai Nairobi Paris Sao Paulo Singapore
Taipei Tokyo Toronto Warsaw

and associated companies in Berlin Ibadan

OXFORD and OXFORD ENGLISH are trade marks of
Oxford University Press

ISBN 0 19 451391 2   International Edition
ISBN 0 19 451397 1   German edition
Bestellnummer: 37495
© Vicki Hollett 1996

First published in the International Edition 1996
Sixth impression 1998
First published in the German Edition 1996
Third impression 1998

Printed in Spain by Mateu Cromo, S.A. Pinto (Madrid)

ACKNOWLEDGEMENTS

*The publisher would like to thank the following for
permission to reproduce photographs:*

ABB Asea Brown Boveri Ltd *p. 30*; AMP of Great Britain Ltd. *p. 140*;
Amstrad *p. 23*; All Nippon Airways Col, Ltd. *p. 30*; Allsport UK Ltd/Al
Bello/Chris Cole/John Gichigi *p. 63*; Aurora/Jose Azel *p. 139*; Aussedat Rey
Group *p. 30*; BICC plc *p. 36*; Carlsberg *p. 30*; Martyn Chillmaid *pp. 24, 42,
78, 85, 130*; Clarion Communications/Coca-Cola *pp. 95,96, 97*; Club Med
p. 110; Eindhoven Foto/Philips *p. 29*; Greg Evans Photo Library *pp. 71, 108,
128, 149*; Facit *p. 52*; Don Glentzer *p. 139*; IBM UK *pp. 28-29*; The Image
Bank/Steve Allen/Marc Romanelli *pp. 38, 126*; Impact Photos *p. 38*; Japan
Airlines *pp. 28-29*; Lex Vehicle Leasing *p. 145*; McDonald's Restaurants Ltd
pp. 34-35; NASDA *p. 50*; Network *p. 83*; Nissan Motor Co. Ltd. *p. 50-51*;
Philips *p. 28-29*; Peugeot Talbot Motor Company Ltd. *p. 146*; Pictor
International Limited *pp. 11, 38, 40, 47, 63, 69, 74, 83, 98, 110, 111, 122,
128, 129, 135*; Pirelli *p. 30*; Rex Features *pp. 108, 126, 128-9*; Karen
Robinson *p. 13*; SABA/Robert Wallis *pp. 35, 116*; Science Photo Library *pp.
38, 147*; Peter Sibbald *p.138*; Tony Stone Images: *pp. 11, 31, 40, 48, 69, 83,
84, 98, 101, 110, 111, 126, 135, 138*; Derek Stirling (courtesy of John Swire
& Sons Ltd) *p15*; Trans World Airlines *p.130*; Zefa Picture Library (UK) Ltd
pp.38, 40, 63, 83, 110

Cover illustration by
Richard Jenkins

Illustrations by:
Peter Clark *p.8*
Jackie Harland *pp. 60, 61, 62*
David Loftus *pp. 12, 15, 58*
Nigel Paige *pp. 14, 21, 56, 65, 70, 93, 114*
Technical Graphics Dept, OUP *pp. 43, 47*

Location photography by
Gareth Boden

Design by
Shireen Nathoo Design

*The authors and publisher are grateful to those who have given
permission to reproduce the following extracts and adaptations
of copyright material:*

p. 13 Adapted from "Mogul in Disguise", by Anil Bhoyrol, © Business Age
Magazine 1994. Reprinted by permission; *p. 15* Profile of Derek Stirling with
kind permission of John Swire & Sons Ltd; *pp. 28-29* Adapted from IBM
Annual Report, with kind permission of © IBM; *pp. 28-29* Taken from Philips
Annual Report, © Philips, by permission; *pp. 28-29* Reproduced with kind
permission of © Japan Airlines; *p. 30* Company Profiles adapted from
Carlsberg A/S 1993/94 Company Report, © Carlsberg, by permission; *p. 30*
Aussedat Rey with kind permission of Marie-Christine Malingre; *p. 30*
Adapted from All Nippon Airways Annual Report 1994 with permission;
p. 30 Adapted from ABB's 1993 Annual Report, by permission; *p. 30*
Reproduced from 1993 Annual Report, © Pirelli; *pp. 34-5* "McDonald's
conquers the world", by Andrew Serwer, © McDonald's; *p. 36* BICC
Company Organisation Chart, © BICC, by permission; *p. 43* Reproduced
from © Cabstar pick-up; *pp. 50-51* Reproduced from © Nissan, by
permission; *p. 52* Reproduced with permission, © Facit (UK) Ltd; *p. 67*
adapted from "Highflying Tastes", with kind permission of © The Daily
Mail/Solo Syndication; *pp. 95-97* "The Chronicle of Coca-Cola since 1886",
© Time Inc. Magazines, by permission. Logo and information reproduced by
kind permission of the Coca-Cola Company; *p. 110* Adapted from Club Med
Summer Brochure (1995); *p. 115* "The Conference Organiser's Brief"
© Metropole Hotels (Holdings) Ltd, by permission; *pp. 121-2* "Comparing
Countries" with kind permission of © The Economist *p. 125* Article "High
living brings stress" by John Harlow, © The Telegraph plc, London, 1995;
p. 130 Reproduced with permission, © TWA; *p. 136* Adapted from "Who's
for lunch" by Alan Leigh, © British Airways Inflight Magazine Business Life;
p. 140 Copyright AMP of Great Britain Ltd 1995; *p. 145* © Lex Vehicle
Leasing; *p. 150* "50 ways to cope with stress", With kind permission of ELTA-
Rhine e.v. Newsletter, January 1994

The author would like to thank the many friends, relatives, colleagues, and
acquaintances who have helped in the writing of this book. Many thanks to
Suren Advani, David Morris, Nigel Newbrook, Bob and Kim Shaw, Toni Witt-
Fox, Brian, Georgie, and Tom Hollett. Too numerous to mention by name are
the many teachers who gave us detailed feedback on the first edition. (Your
comments were invaluable and we hope you like the result.) I'm also grateful
to EF Language Schools and Emma Tanner, Liz Lyon, Roger Carter, Rick
Baldwin, Michael Black, and all the staff at EFI Cambridge for their ideas and
help in piloting.